Praise for

My Father's Business

"Similar to Walmart, Cal Turner and his dad built their retail business based on the small-town values of hard work, perseverance, family, and faith. *My Father's Business* is the story of what it took to build Dollar General into a national retail chain from its rural, Kentucky roots, and it will encourage anyone with a dream of building a business."　　　　—Doug McMillon, president and CEO, Walmart

"The Dollar General story is not only a great American business success story, it is also a love story of a family that cares deeply for each other, their team, and their customers. This classic story told through the eyes of my friend Cal Jr. is instructive in almost every area of life. I simply could not put it down. Must-read!"

—Dave Ramsey, bestselling author and
nationally syndicated radio show host

"*My Father's Business* is a *must-read* for an aspiring young entrepreneur and an enjoyable read for anyone."

—Dr. Thomas Frist, co-founder,
Hospital Corporation of America

"*My Father's Business* ought to be required reading in any business school interested in the incredible growth of a business from a two-man start-up to a public *Fortune* 300 company. *My Father's Business* is a good read with a lot of important commonsense advice....A great book!"

—Peter Handal, president and CEO,
Dale Carnegie Training

"This book is a gripping account of a godly man who built a great institution to serve others. It contains both leadership and business lessons. Anyone aspiring to lead, learn, and create enormous value will benefit from this book."

—L. Jay Bourgeois, III, professor of
Business Strategy, senior fellow
and former director, Darden Center
for Global Initiatives, Darden School of
Business, University of Virginia

"Cal lives the Dollar General mission statement, 'Serving Others.' His small-town roots and spirituality emphasize valuing every person and appreciating the challenges of the Dollar General customer. *My Father's Business* describes the path on which Cal has walked while 'Serving Others' along the way."

—David M. Wilds, managing partner,
First Avenue Partners, L.P.

"This is a fantastic book, for new entrepreneurs and CEOs alike, and it will inspire pastors, teachers, not-for-profit organizations, and everyone who wants to integrate personal aspirations, family values, and best business practices."

—Rev. Dr. Becca Stevens, founder and
president, Thistle Farms

"From the challenges and opportunities of the Dollar General story, *My Father's Business* allows anyone aspiring to lead with heart, mind, and soul to imagine what is possible."

—Bishop Bill McAlilly,
Nashville Episcopal Area of the
United Methodist Church

"This isn't a book about humble beginnings. It is about humility. *My Father's Business* follows a spiritual journey that leads to a life lived inward and outward—from youth to retirement. That is success. That has been Cal's business. That is the business we all should be in."

—John F. Kutsko, executive director, the Society of
Biblical Literature and Affiliate Faculty at
the Candler School of Theology, Emory University

"Reading Cal's book gave me further insight into the founding of Dollar General by his grandfather and father. Cal's deep sense of conviction to carry out the strong traditions set by these two great Americans is inspirational. My personal experience with a great retailer allows me a deep appreciation for what Cal's family and company accomplished. It is great to read and enjoy a book written by a fellow 'Backsliding Methodist.'"

—Barney Barnett, vice chairman,
Publix Super Markets Inc.

My Father's Business

The Small-Town Values That Built
Dollar General into a Billion-Dollar Company

Cal Turner, Jr.
with Rob Simbeck

CENTER
STREET

NEW YORK   NASHVILLE

Center Street
Hachette Book Group
1290 Avenue of the Americas, New York, NY 10104
centerstreet.com
twitter.com/centerstreet

First published in hardcover, ebook, and as a special trade paperback in May 2018.
This Trade Paperback Edition: April 2019

Center Street is a division of Hachette Book Group, Inc. The Center Street name and logo are trademarks of Hachette Book Group, Inc.

The publisher is not responsible for websites (or their content) that are not owned by the publisher.

The Hachette Speakers Bureau provides a wide range of authors for speaking events. To find out more, go to www.HachetteSpeakersBureau.com or call (866) 376-6591.

Library of Congress Cataloging-in-Publication Data has been applied for.

ISBNs: 978-1-4789-9296-7 (trade paperback), 978-1-4789-9299-8 (ebook)

Printed in the United States of America

LSC-C

10 9 8 7 6 5 4 3 2 1

I dedicate this book to you, the reader, that you may be emboldened in your pursuit of your Father's business.

CONTENTS

ACKNOWLEDGMENTS

I have been blessed with family, friends, and coworkers as sources of love and inspiration. I hope this book makes clear that I am deeply grateful to them.

My father believed anyone would do well to be brought up in a small town, and I am grateful for my upbringing in Scottsville, Kentucky. My wife, Margaret, is also the product of a small Kentucky town, Park City, and she has, among many other things, made me a more complete person and better able to relate to others. I consider her to have lovingly accepted the handoff from my mother.

I am grateful to the thousands of company partners, especially those working in the stores and warehouses, who helped make Dollar General Corporation a family. Just as my grandmother was the strength behind my grandfather, and my mother was the strength and anchor behind my father, the women who were the vast majority of our store managers and customers were the backbone of the company. They taught me the relationship essence of leadership. Still, no one embodied our customers more in terms of my story than the old farmer who bought a 39-cent pair of panties from me when I was a store clerk at Allen Dry Goods in 1953. He first taught me to understand our business from the perspective of struggling, hardworking customers.

My thanks to Rob Simbeck, who urged me to tell my story and helped me shape it, and our agent, Leah Spiro, who guided us expertly through the proposal and negotiation process, and helped make this a better book. Thanks to the Hachette team for its enthusiastic embrace of this book and its efforts to make it everything it could be: Rolf Zettersten, for partnering with us; Christina Boys and Hannah Phillips, for their wonderful editorial guidance; Ed Crawford, for the cover art and design; Patsy Jones in marketing; and Billy Clark and Gina Wynn in sales.

As always, I am grateful to Avalee Suneima, an incredible assistant who, strangely enough, has learned to think as I do, sometimes *before* I do.

INTRODUCTION

The family business that would one day become Dollar General Corporation came into existence in October 1939 as J. L. Turner and Son Wholesale Dry Goods, Shoes, Notions and Hosiery. I was born three months later as Hurley Calister Turner, Jr., and I've always considered us to be a joint venture.

That "Jr." meant my role as the boss's son was clearly laid out from the start. In my mind, my dad was and always will be "the real Cal Turner."

My life has embodied many seeming contradictions. I thought about the ministry even before I thought about business as a career. I stepped into a family enterprise with its roots in a farmers' co-op and retired from a Fortune 300 company with almost 6,000 stores, 60,000 employees, and $6 billion in annual sales. Although my dad and I were alike in many ways and he was my biggest supporter and closest friend, we had what may have been inevitable father-son disagreements that ultimately involved the board and led to his forced retirement as chairman of the board of the company he had founded and nurtured.

My years with the company changed me a great deal. Among other things, they made me a passionate believer in human development, in the kind of leadership that makes better organizations by shaping better persons, something that dovetails nicely with the small-town values imbued in me by my family and the community of Scottsville, Kentucky.

This book is about my journey of self-discovery and is my attempt to share what I've learned about how all of us can flourish and how we can best work together for the good of organizations, communities, and our world. I hope that within it you will find keys to exploring your own life and becoming everything you are capable of being as you pursue your Father's business.

1

❧

Scottsville, Kentucky: "The Center of the Universe"

Scottsville, Kentucky, was a great place for a kid to grow up, but it was a terrible place for a wholesale business. Nashville, 60 miles to the south, or Louisville, 120 miles to the north, would have been much better. Fewer than 2,000 people lived in Scottsville in 1939, and the roads leading in and out were winding and rutted. To my father and my grandfather, though, Scottsville was the center of the universe. Besides, they had just bought a big brick building on East Main Street—they had gotten it for half price, and a Turner will buy *anything* for half price—and so Scottsville it was.

My grandfather, James Luther Turner, was one of the smartest men I have ever known. He was also one of the hardest working. He was just eleven when his father died in a freak wrestling accident in 1902, and as the oldest of four children, he left school to run the family farm. I picture him in those days as a skinny kid walking behind their mule, turning up dusty Macon County, Tennessee, dirt so he could plant corn for the hogs, vegetables for the family, and tobacco for cash.

He sold his first tobacco crop for $190 and put part of the money into savings. When he said, as he often did, "You need to save something from every paycheck," it was because he had done it and had learned that it worked. From the beginning, he dreamed of a better life, and at twenty-four, he was asked to manage the local co-op by farmers who recognized him as the hardest-working young man around. He had by that time saved $300, and he opened a bridle shop in a refurbished woodshed behind the co-op, which amounted to a general store, making and selling bridles, harnesses, and saddles in his spare time. He would set out on foot before dawn, carrying a lunch as he walked the three miles from the farm to the co-op, and walk back at night.

He and his wife, Josiephine—they married when he was seventeen—lost two children in infancy, and they devoted themselves tirelessly to their third and only surviving child, Hurley Calister, born May 28, 1915. Hurley was the surname of a prominent area man, and my grandmother, whose own name was spelled with a country flourish, just liked the sound of "Calister."

Luther worked at the co-op for about a year—after running his own farm, he wasn't much for bosses. He and his brother-in-law bought the inventory of a small general store and used it to start their own in Adolphus, across the state line in Allen County, Kentucky. In 1920, just after Luther bought a second store, the nation entered a severe recession. His stores failed, and he figured it was time to try working for someone else again.

He approached Nashville's Dobson-Cannon Wholesale Grocery Company, which was less than impressed with his third-grade education but hired him as a salesman when he offered to work on straight commission. "Just give me your sales sheets and pay me for what I sell," he told them. A year later, he jumped at the chance to work for Neely Harwell, a Nashville dry goods wholesaler. He loaded samples of their merchandise into his car and showed them to store owners all over southern Kentucky and middle Tennessee. A natural salesman, he flourished, although he never lost the dream of returning to his own business. In the meantime, he learned all he could and saved his money.

It says a great deal about Luther Turner that he was able to turn his third-grade education into a plus. He was convinced that everyone he met was smarter than he, and that he needed to learn something from each of them. He became a first-rate observer, a great listener, and a dedicated student of life. What he practiced was more than empathy. It involved valuing the other person and his or her information, insight, and perspective.

With a steady job and a son who had just turned ten, Luther decided the family needed the advantages of a town. The closest one was Scottsville, and that's where they moved. Luther found and bought the cheapest house on the best street in town, putting his wife and son in the finest surroundings he could afford.

Living on $125 of the $225 he earned monthly from Neely Harwell, Luther used the rest to open Turner's Bargain Store on South Court Street. That was where Cal, who helped out when he could, took his first independent step into the world of retail in the summer of 1929. He and his friend Howard Shrum, whose father owned the shoe store next door, teamed up and sold lemonade on the sidewalk. It was all you could drink for a nickel. They gave people plenty of ice, knowing that the colder the lemonade, the better the chance their customers, gulping in the hot summer sun, would get a "brain freeze" after half a glass or so. Cal and Howard couldn't help it if "all you can drink" didn't turn out to be very much. They made $12.

A few months later, Black Friday kicked off the Great Depression. It would be much worse than the downturn of a decade earlier, but Luther was much better prepared. His years on the road, in and out of the little department stores found in nearly every town, had taught him volumes. He had seen the business as a wholesaler and a retailer, from the perspectives of owners and customers, in good times and bad. He knew their merchandise, their cash flows, their strengths and weaknesses. He was by this time part psychologist, part philosopher, and all businessman.

When the Depression hit, Cal was in eighth grade, which meant he had completed four more years of schooling than his father. He was especially good with numbers, and Luther began taking him on the road.

Cal was a quick study. He picked up on what made customers' eyes light up and what left them cold. No one in those little towns had much money. They wanted value and knew how to spot it.

Luther saw that many of these stores weren't going to make it. They had mortgages, utilities, vendors, and other creditors to pay, but their customers lacked cash, so they simply couldn't move their merchandise at anything close to what they had in it. What had happened to him and his two little stores in the early twenties was happening all over the rural South in the thirties. He also knew that where there was failure, there was opportunity. He had opened that first store with merchandise from a failed retailer. Here was the chance to do that with store after store. Someone would be buying the merchandise at bargain-basement prices, on the courthouse steps if nowhere else. It might as well be Luther.

In photos from that era, with his suit and tie, slim build, and glasses, Luther looked like a young Harry Truman. But behind the glasses, there was a fatherless farm boy who started with nothing, facing the early days of the worst depression in the country's history. If there was ever a test of a man's mettle and a nation's promise, this was it, but it was clear that he had already come a great distance from his days of walking behind a mule in that Tennessee dirt.

As the Depression deepened, Luther began buying the inventories of failed stores, often competing with other bidders to do so. He and Cal would show up early on auction day, and Cal learned quickly from Luther how to size up merchandise and assign value. It helped that Cal was a whiz with numbers. He'd walk around with a pad and pencil, listing items and doing the figuring.

"I count sixty-two pairs of shoes," Cal might say, "and it looks like an average price of a dollar twenty-five." He'd go through as much as he could this way—sacks of sugar, baby dresses, rolls of wallpaper, whatever they had—writing his approximations on a note pad. He might determine that the entire stock was worth $4,500, and Luther would try to buy it for $2,000 or so. My father is no longer here to ask, but I wonder now whether my practical grandfather took cash with him to those sales, since that seems most logical—he was, after all, a stranger at many of them.

When theirs was the winning bid, Luther would liquidate the stock quickly, holding a "going out of business" sale, sometimes hiring someone to handle it, sometimes staying on to do it himself, with Cal at his side. Anything that didn't sell he could pack up and take to his own store in Scottsville or sell to another retailer. Now and then he would scout around for another merchant or middleman and sell the whole lot at a small markup. And on a couple of rare occasions, where he thought with the right manager he could turn a store around, he simply bought it outright.

Sometimes he needed short-term bank loans to make the purchases, and the banks were more than happy to work with him. His track record spoke for itself. He used the stock as collateral, and they knew they'd have their money back in sixty or ninety days. He was "bankable" in a way that farmers, whose crops might not come in, were not. At other times, he would take on a short-term partner. They would buy a store together, with a handshake as the only contract. They would divide the goods as evenly as possible and flip a coin to see who got what.

Those sales helped make a businessman of young Cal. As he and his dad went from store to store, month after month and year after year, he became more like a partner than simply a helpful son, even though he was still in high school.

In fact, my dad did very well at Scottsville High, even finding time to become a terrific basketball player, all while keeping up a sometimes daunting work schedule in the bargain store and in another that Luther owned thirty-five miles away in Hartsville, Tennessee. My dad would often get up early on Saturday mornings to make the drive and spend the day, and sometimes the evening, at the store. There were also times when he would leave the house with Luther as early as 1:00 a.m. to drive to a bankruptcy sale.

Meanwhile, Turner's Bargain Store continued to do well. The importance of tobacco as a local crop gave my grandfather one of his best early promotional opportunities. Farmers sold their tobacco late in the fall, receiving checks they turned into the only cash many of them saw all year. Luther knew those sale barns were cold and he came up with the idea of giving each farmer at those sales a good right-hand work glove with a note attached. It said, "Get the mate to me free at Turner's Bargain Store. We will gladly cash your check." The farmers would go to the store and get the mate to a good pair of gloves, then cash their checks. There they'd be, inside a store loaded with useful merchandise, with a year's worth of crop money in their hands.

Cal enrolled at Vanderbilt University in Nashville in the fall of 1933 to study engineering. The only admission requirement was Luther's ability to pay the tuition.

Given their humble beginnings, Luther and Josie were thrilled that their son was earning a college degree, and they bought a house on Villa Place, just a few blocks from the school. My dad played on the freshman basketball team, but quickly discovered engineering wasn't for him. School in general didn't interest him anymore. Business did. After his freshman year, he took what his parents thought was a summer job at Neely Harwell. Then, as fall approached, he broke it to them that he wasn't going back to school.

On the side, my dad opened a store of his own in Dupontonia, a DuPont company town on the Cumberland River north of Nashville. Since he was a good fellow and his prices were right, he felt he deserved people's business. The locals didn't see it that way and it went under. Luther, who was not averse to letting Cal learn some of his lessons the hard way, simply watched from the sidelines. Then, the two of them went back to the business of buying and liquidating the inventories of troubled stores.

My dad was dating Laura Katherine Goad, who was a year behind him in high school. She came from a family of lawyers and politicians on one side and businesspeople on the other. In a social sense, the Goads were above the station of the Turners, no matter how far they had come from that Tennessee farm. The Goads would produce judges and politicians, while the Kemps—her mother's side—owned a store. But Cal, good-looking, dapper, and filled with self-confidence, thought he could accomplish pretty much anything, including winning Laura.

He still carried some of the earthiness that went with the family's rural background, and that wasn't always an endearing trait. Once, when he and Laura broke up for a short time, my dad got a date with her rival, Lattie Miller Graves, the doctor's daughter. The two of them drove by Laura's house in his new convertible with the top down and the radio blaring. Fortunately, my mother later decided to take him back, but I'm convinced that if her father hadn't died when he did—in an automobile accident at the age of forty-two, when my mother was eighteen—she would never have married him. The Turners were uneducated farm people who had moved into town, and my guess is that Luther Turner's young son, Cal, would not have been good enough for Frank Goad's only daughter. As it was, her joyfulness and free spirit and his charm and confidence made for a great match. One of their favorite pastimes was to drive out to the bridge on Gallatin Road south of town, park the car, turn up the radio, and dance, high above the creek below.

They married on October 24, 1936. Daddy was as proud of their first child, Laura Josephine, born December 26, 1937, as of anything he'd ever done, and one day he took her into the store and set her lovingly atop a display pile of fabric. As the customers gathered around, she wet herself, soaking both her diaper and the cloth.

The Depression hadn't lifted, but the newlyweds entered a world in which the economic landscape had at least stabilized. Unemployment had dropped from nearly 25 percent in 1933 to 17 percent in 1939. It was possible to see who had outlasted the storm. Those retailers who remained needed goods, and it was my dad who had the idea of going into wholesaling. At twenty-four, he had learned his father's lessons well and had saved $5,000—equivalent to nearly $90,000 today. He knew he needed more, so he asked Luther for $5,000 as well. The building that had been offered for sale in Scottsville would be a great location, the price was right, and Luther said yes. With that, they were in the wholesale business.

J. L. Turner and Son began selling to independent retailers in Kentucky and Tennessee. Cal ordered and brought in stock, and hit the road with his samples on selling trips. By the end of the first year, he had sold $65,000 worth of goods, and they were off and running.

The founding of J. L. Turner and Son followed by less than sixty days the German invasion of Poland and the onset of World War II. President Roosevelt signed into law the first peacetime draft in U.S. history a year later, but my birth in January 1940 made my dad the father of two, and as such, he would never be subject to the draft. Instead, he and my grandfather did what they could to thrive during the austere wartime economy. They concentrated on what my father always figured he did best—finding great bargains and selling them to retailers—supplementing the money they made wholesaling with income from their remaining retail outlets and a few side projects, including a tomato cannery in Scottsville. I still remember the Allen's Pride label on those cans and the sickly, pungent smell of the place!

In the boom following the war, manufacturers freed up from

wartime production began flooding the market with all sorts of commodities, driving prices down. My father found more and more deals he just couldn't resist, passing them along to his retail customers. At one point he found a bargain on a huge volume of ladies' panties, which he shipped to the warehouse. He took samples to his customers and found they weren't buying, since they still had plenty of the *last* batch of panties he'd sold them.

"But these are even cheaper!" he said. "Lower your prices and you'll sell more of them!"

He was touting a new business approach, but his customers, a conservative lot, weren't buying his argument or his panties. It began happening more and more. My dad, who couldn't pass up a bargain, would end up with way too much of something. The storeowners who were ideally a pipeline to customers were instead a bottleneck.

If he couldn't move that lot of panties through those other retail stores, my dad figured it was time for him and his father to open more stores of their own, so they could complement his aggressive buying with some smart selling. He put it another way years later, saying, "We realized you had to go directly to the consumer. We decided we had to have more outlets to get rid of our mistakes."

The initial idea, he said, was "selling the good stuff to the rich folks, but we were late getting into retailing and Mr. Karl Stark was already doing that in Scottsville. So we had to sell the cheap stuff to the poor folks. It was just the business we had to get into."

It was also the business they knew best. They were acquainted with retailers and would-be retailers throughout Kentucky and Tennessee, and they found willing partners. They knew they couldn't run these "junior department stores" themselves. Local businessmen would manage the stores. The Turners would provide wholesale merchandise. They would lease the buildings jointly with the local managers and split the profits as fifty-fifty partners. If either party wanted out, he would declare the value of the store and the other could buy or sell at that price. My dad was convinced that any genuine partnership needed two persons completely and equally committed to success. It also needed a mutually agreeable exit strategy from the beginning.

The first store opened with such a partnership was in Albany, Kentucky—Albany Dry Goods. Then they added a store in Horse Cave and, in 1948, Russell Springs. One at a time, they added others, and within a few years, they had a dozen.

One of those new stores was Allen Dry Goods, on the square in Scottsville. The building had become available when Karl Stark finally got out of the business. Like our short-lived cannery business, it was named for Allen County, which had Scottsville as its county seat. This one was solely owned rather than the kind of partnership Dad and Luther normally negotiated.

From the beginning, my dad ran the business and Luther served as loving mentor—and worrier. In fact, Cal's hunger for growth, for more and more stores, worried Luther a great deal. Cal had a young man's ambition. Luther, in his mid-fifties, had an older man's caution. At one point, Luther bought a farm and put it in Josiephine's name so that if the company went under, all of them could return to the land and start over.

Cal did heed Luther's concerns—he told me he often woke up in a cold sweat, wondering whether they were overextended—but Luther listened to Cal as well. They would ride together to Nashville to visit Sam Flemming, the credit manager at Third National Bank, and Luther would always provide the needed second signature for a loan that would let them launch another store.

That business, growing one store at a time, was the backdrop to my childhood. The fact that it was headquartered in Scottsville pleased my father, who was convinced that living in a small town made you a better person.

"If people are keeping an eye on what you're doing," he said, "then you might think twice about doing something you shouldn't."

I grew up knowing that *everyone* kept an eye on me. Since my mother came from a family of lawyers and politicians, she was always very visible and involved in the community. That made me visible as well. Mama was part of every school project, and our house was open to anyone who wanted to visit or anyone we wanted to bring home, announced or unannounced.

Mama drummed into me from the time I was little that I needed to reach out and connect with everyone, to be interested and respectful no matter what. I learned to share my toys, to like people from all walks of life, to be friendly and polite at all times. I have felt her influence ever since, urging me to understand people, to help them all I can, and to try to make them feel better about themselves and their potential. In fact, many years later, when my son was seven, he said, "Daddy, it's hard to be your son, because you have to be nice to everybody all the time, whether you feel like it or not." It was just part of small-town life that always stayed with me, and it became one of the strengths of my leadership grounding.

My mother was love in action. She found a way to respect and appreciate everyone, and she was fun loving in a way that involved all those around her. She lived life at a brisk pace, with a wholesome but frisky sense of humor. Mama had grown up with three brothers, one older and two younger, and had learned how to handle the men in her life. You knew you were acting as she wanted, but you were more than happy to comply. I know I was.

Mama was very much the Southern lady. She was a pretty woman with dark brown hair, blue eyes, and a fair complexion. She was a great homemaker and cook, but no matter how busy the day had been, she met my father at the door just out of the bath, wearing fresh lipstick and looking her absolute best. She'd greet him with a big hug, and I give her a lot of the credit for the fact that they remained sweethearts throughout their lives.

My dad was the boss at work; she was the boss at home. She'd let him fume and bluster now and then if he wanted to assert control about something, knowing he'd calm down soon enough, but when he had his way, it was probably because she let him.

Mama was the spiritual center of every gathering. She made a big deal out of everyone's birthday. At Christmas, the decorations were festive and homey and the house always smelled heavenly. For days, she would boil orange peels for a fruity, spiced tea she made, and she was always baking something special. The house we moved into when I was thirteen was a big colonial with six white columns, and Mama would wrap red ribbon around each, making them look like peppermint candy. She saw to it that there was a big meal for every occasion, and I'll never forget her banana cake with homemade custard between layers.

She found a recipe for brandied peaches one year in the Louisville paper, and filled gallon jugs with peaches, sugar, and spices, and buried them in the yard for a month. There were so many, she lost track of some of them, and sometime after Easter, when the weather got really warm, we began hearing muffled explosions in the yard.

"Oh, yes," she'd say, "now I remember one being buried over there." It was just part of the adventure.

At Halloween, ours was a must-stop house for everyone—three or four hundred people would come by! Mama would make homemade chili and tamales to entice the entire family to come and eat and then help pass out candy to the seemingly endless line of trick-or-treaters.

Where my mother's family was all about community and civic involvement, my father's stuck to business. He was gone much of the time and so Mama was the bigger influence on Laura Jo, me, and our two younger siblings, Betty (Katherine Elizabeth) and Steve (James

Stephen). During my formative years, my dad was too busy to have much rapport with me. The only time we really spent together when I was little was when I'd visit stores with him. I was five the first time and I remember how excited I was when he said, "I want Cal Jr. to go with me to visit stores today." I thought I had arrived! That emotion was quickly replaced by fear once we got on the road, however, because his driving scared the heck out of me! It was a thrill just to get to each store in one piece. Once we were there, he'd start talking shop with managers and employees, and I'd get bored in a hurry. There isn't much interesting about a retail store to a preschooler.

We didn't have most of the normal father-son venues for a relationship; it was simply a consequence of the way he had grown up. His father was functionally illiterate and needed him as a functionary in the business enterprise, so business was their connection, just as it became ours.

I heard a *lot* of business talk as a kid. We'd be in the living room waiting for Grandma to finish cooking Sunday dinner, and I'd listen as my father and my grandfather talked about retailing. Looking back, I realize that the two of them had a great deal of affection for each other, but you had to hear it through the constant chatter about shipments and bargains and overhead.

I remember a discussion of one of their more memorable promotions. For a time they sold a shoe line, specially made for the company, called Turson, a contraction of Turner and Son. My dad wanted to promote it at the county fair in Scottsville one year, so he had one of the shoes frozen in a big block of ice, which was set out in the sun. He announced a prize for the person who could guess the time at which the ice would be melted enough for the shoe to drop to the ground. It was just the kind of homey, small-town touch he knew would work, and he certainly got his money's worth when it came to that crowd.

My grandmother was the hardest-working lady I ever met. To her, a meal was two or three meats, a half-dozen vegetables, cornbread, biscuits, and at least two desserts, and she could do all that with very little advance notice. She canned fruits and vegetables from her garden, kept a spotless house, and quilted, knitted, and crocheted.

I still remember her kneeling beside her bed and saying her prayers at night. She would be deeply engrossed, speaking in an emotional mumble that was very moving to me. I remember talking to her once about the fact that since Daddy didn't go to church, I didn't really know where he stood with God. The Baptist in her came out as she said, "I'll have you know your dad has been saved. He's all right."

There was never anything fancy about her. I don't think she had as much education as my grandfather—many children left school in those days in favor of farm work—but her level of sophistication didn't matter. I deeply respected her contribution to the family.

I respected my grandfather's, too, but despite his native intelligence, his lack of education showed every time he spoke. I can't recall a grammatical error he didn't make. He had an organized mind and invariably made the point he wanted to make, but his poor grammar embarrassed me when I was young. My mother was an advocate of correct grammar, and her example helped smooth my dad's rough edges when it came to expressing himself, but she was able just to accept her father-in-law the way he was. I loved him, I respected him, I knew he was my dad's mentor and advisor, but I had a problem with the way he butchered the language. That would lessen for me through the years, and my memories of his keen insight into people and business have long since outweighed my childish sensitivity to that minor flaw.

2

✧

The Lessons of Adolescence

The warehouse in Scottsville did double duty, since it also housed the company's offices. You could look up from your desk, if you had one, and see people pulling orders, gathering merchandise from piles and stacks that seemed to have no real rhyme or reason.

There were just a handful of employees at first, including Howard Cole, who served as bookkeeper and credit manager, and James Gordon Wilson, a salesman who stayed on the road most of the time. Leo Allen came on board in 1946 as a driver, hauling merchandise in his own truck. His first trip for the company was to Louisville with a load of leather jackets. There was no loading dock in those days, so Leo backed up to the front porch and loaded or unloaded from there.

Early on, my dad had the only office, in the middle of the front of the warehouse. Howard's desk was nearby, in a kind of bullpen, along with those of Marie Gerald and Anna Lois Landrum. Anna sat on an old wrought iron ice cream parlor chair, and it must not have looked very comfortable, because "Miss Josie," my grandmother, made a blue cushion and brought it to her. My dad was not the kind of man to spend extra money for such things.

One day an office furniture salesman named Harry Bowman came in from Bowling Green and saw Howard sitting at his old desk on a wire-framed Coca-Cola chair with a cotton-padded pillow on it. He showed Howard his company's best model, a "Cadillac of office chairs." Yes, Howard agreed, it was big and beautiful, but it cost sixty bucks in 1948 dollars. Howard told Harry he could get by with what he had, and when my dad walked by, Howard told him so too. So he was surprised when my dad studied the chair for a minute.

"If Cal Turner puts a dime in a Coke machine," Howard said later, "he's on his toes until the Coke actually comes out. Cal can trust his judgment, but he can't trust that machine."

But my dad, a born wheeler-dealer with an eye for value and a knowledge of the marketplace, said, "Harry, that chair couldn't have cost your company more than thirty-five dollars. I'll tell you what. Let's flip a coin. If I win, I pay you thirty-five. If you win, I pay you sixty." Harry agreed and that thirty-five-dollar chair lasted for more than twenty-five years.

As Luther got older, he began sliding toward dementia. I first realized something wasn't right as he and I drove the back roads toward the farm in his Pontiac. He would begin mumbling, and the few words I could make out let me know he was talking with an imaginary someone about business. I would say something to him and eventually he would come around, but it was very disconcerting and it certainly didn't help his driving, which became more and more erratic. He began to prefer the middle of the road, which frightened the rest of the family as much as it frightened me. In fact, it scared pretty much everyone in town. Meanwhile, it added greatly to the burden my father bore. He was already consumed entirely with the company's business, and he now had the added emotional strain of grieving the loss of the father who had been his partner. The fact that Luther was still alive in no way eased his load. Cal was now in every way sole proprietor.

As my father took on even more responsibilities, I began hearing about *his* health as well.

"We're worried about how hard your father is working," people told me time after time. "We're afraid he's going to have a heart attack."

I knew that my grandfather had to take over the farm when he was eleven because his father had died young, and here I was, almost eleven, hearing that my dad was on the brink.

My dad would laugh it off.

"Hard work won't kill you," he'd say. "It really is good for you!" I found that hard to believe, and it was a doubly scary prospect because of my name—as Cal Jr., I was next in line.

In fact, I always carried great expectations, even as a child. I was the number one son, as my brother, Steve, was seven years younger. No matter what happened, it seemed I could take care of things, and I was asked to handle difficult communications at a very young age. As my grandfather continued to slip, my parents decided someone should talk to him, and they knew he listened when I spoke—I was the one who spent the most time with him. Mama asked me to bring up the subject of his driving. I never did work up the nerve to do it, and he finally stopped before anyone was hurt. Still, it was quite a bit of responsibility to give an eleven-year-old, but it's reflective of the way my parents viewed their older son.

The age of eleven was also a turning point for me in a spiritual sense. Part of being a good boy in a small town was going to church regularly, and I remember when attending out of obedience and expectation turned into a more adult form of spirituality. My faith became very real after one Sunday evening youth fellowship meeting. I was waiting for my parents to pick me up, sitting on the porch of my uncle's house across the street from the church in the lovely summer twilight. Suddenly, the words to "The Old Rugged Cross" came over me with real impact. The message at that moment was not so much that Jesus had died for the whole world, but that he had died specifically for Cal Turner, Jr. I had never felt anything like it. I felt the touch of Christ and knew I was going to be different from that moment on. I had no idea what that meant, but I knew I'd been changed. It was not about being religious. It was about that relationship. To this day, religion that takes the form of exclusivity, judgmentalism, and church bureaucracy is a turnoff to me. Jesus Christ has always been and will continue to be a turn-on.

The fact that "The Old Rugged Cross" played such a profound role in my spiritual awakening points to the importance of music in my life. My mother's side of the family provided the musical background, although it's a wonder I learned to love music so much, given my early lessons. My first teacher was my aunt Ruth, who lived next door. She was pretty and petite, with brown hair and blue eyes, and although she claimed shyness, she was very outspoken. She was very good at loving from a distance—she would voice approval of me to others—but I never heard or felt it.

She would lie in her gown on the couch smoking cigarettes during my piano lessons, calling out the correct note when I played the wrong one. Then, she would walk across the room and hover over me. Anytime I hit a wrong note, she would hit my finger with a pencil. The fear was self-fulfilling. "That pencil's going to come down any second," I would think, and the tension would, as often as not, send my finger in an errant direction and bring the pencil down on it. I learned soon enough to avoid her. I would go out the front door at lesson time, circle around to the shed in back of the house, and hide. When the time for the lesson had passed, I'd go back in the house.

"How was your lesson, son?" my mother would ask.

"It was good," I'd say.

That worked until the time for a recital got close and both Aunt Ruth and I knew I wasn't ready. My mother finally realized Aunt Ruth and I had a problem and she let me quit taking lessons. Later, another neighbor, Frances Read, a character in her own right, taught me. She was a beautiful woman who dressed to the nines every day. She would come down her stairs wearing a big diamond ring, and when she sat next to me, I could smell the Listerine on her breath. She seemed troubled, but I would do anything for her. A well-trained musician, she had attended the exclusive Ward Belmont School in Nashville, and her beauty was accompanied by a kind, supportive approach—pretty much the opposite of Aunt Ruth's. I practiced hard and learned a great deal from her.

I think the contrast in style between Aunt Ruth and Mrs. Read was an influence on my management style. I performed so much better with Mrs. Read, whose elegance and dignified approach affirmed me, than with Aunt Ruth, who neither affirmed me nor seemed to enjoy her role as piano teacher.

My mother knew better than to give me lessons, even though she played beautifully. A parent can't usually teach a child to play piano, and my mother didn't fancy herself a teacher anyway. Her mother had been a natural at the piano, playing by ear from the time she was a little girl. In fact, she would come into her father's store in Hartsville, Tennessee, and demonstrate the Baldwin pianos he had in stock. Her playing helped sell quite a few of them.

I was thirteen the first time I played the organ for Sunday morning worship, in a church with no air-conditioning—just a ceiling fan. I was playing "Holy, Holy, Holy," hymn No. 1 in the Methodist hymnal, and the hymnal page started moving because of the fan, so I began blowing on it to counteract the effect. I was playing along, blowing on the music, when I looked up at the mirror above the music rack and saw Lawrence Bishop, my dad's renegade lumberman friend, in the back of the church, laughing himself silly. I realized what I must have looked like, but it was the only way to keep the music in place. It was a pretty inauspicious beginning, but it helped launch a lifelong love of music and the arts.

My father's long business-related absences meant my mother remained our chief disciplinarian as I approached my teenage years. Growing up in a house full of boys taught her the need for discipline, and she set the family routines, rotating monthly chores and privileges between Laura Jo, Betty, and me (Steve was still too young) in a way designed to help minimize conflict. Whoever washed dishes got first choice when it came to matters like who sat in the front seat of the car or who got the first turn at something. Whoever dried dishes got second choice, and whoever swept the floor got third. Those chores rotated every month. It worked like a charm—there was never anything to argue about!—until one day my dad came home from work and made an announcement that set up one of the few real clashes between my parents.

"Cal Jr.," he said, "is not going to be doing any more women's work."

In that instant, I was absolved of my domestic chores. That, of course, did not go over well with my mother or my sisters. They were angry and the atmosphere was chilly for quite a while. I would have been much happier to continue doing the chores just to keep things going smoothly, and actually, I think part of the reason Mama didn't like it was that I was probably her best worker (in my humble opinion!). But from then on, I worked in the warehouse or in the store rather than at home. Gradually—very gradually—the storm passed.

Mama was good at keeping us in line because when she said something, she meant it. She had big, expressive eyes and could accomplish a lot with just a look. She didn't need to say a word to convey that we needed to shape up. She could also be marvelously subtle. If I scowled in concentration as I listened to someone, looking as though I were annoyed when she knew that wasn't the case, she would say, "Cal Jr., you're out of touch with your face again." If we misbehaved too much, she'd get out the hairbrush and put the back of it to our backsides or get a switch—leaves on the end—and switch the backs of our legs. If it got serious, she'd say, "Your father will deal with this when he gets home." We'd spend the day dreading his arrival, and then he'd dread having to discipline us. He hated it as much as we did, although that didn't stop him from reaching for his belt.

My mother knew I was a sensitive child. I wanted to please everybody and was perhaps too concerned with what other people thought. I was very serious—born old, she would say—and I so wanted everything to be all right for other folks that I'd sometimes want to protect them from themselves. When my teenage sister wanted to borrow a quarter from me, I'd say no because I knew she was going to buy cigarettes and I didn't think she should. I was prim and proper to the point where Mama warned me about being too "prissy." She wanted me to be more natural around people, something that came very easily for her. She always had a terrific sense of humor, perhaps even better than my dad's, and she thought of life and people as worth laughing about. She carried that humor all through her life, and she wanted me to be able to laugh at myself.

She was never hesitant about offering guidance or correction she thought might help me improve or understand human nature better. "Cal Jr.," she said, "I'm going to tell you what hurts because I love you. Your friends will only talk about you behind your back, and the truth will be hard to come by. I have a different kind of commitment to you than your friends do."

She knew, as my father did, that some people would talk about us because we were better off than many people in town. I learned from her that it went with the territory and wasn't worth getting upset about. Dad's comment was, "People will forgive you for anything before they'll forgive you for being successful."

My parents loved us enough to try to imbue us with values they felt would serve us far better than restrictive controls. They believed in us, and we developed belief in ourselves, and that was the most productive growth influence we could have had.

One part of my youth that helped build self-confidence was summer camp, although the experience had a memorably rocky start.

When I was nine, Mama and Daddy sent me to Camp Daniel Boone in Lexington, Kentucky. I hated it. I'd never spent time away from home and I got unbelievably homesick, especially when it was my turn to put on the gloves in boxing class. In fact, I got physically ill. After four long, miserable days, someone from the camp called my parents, who came and got me.

My mother was determined to help me lick my homesickness, and she began looking for another camp. She heard about Camp Dunroamin near Fayetteville, Tennessee, from a woman who worked at Burke's Department Store in Nashville. The woman told her how wonderful the camp and the people who ran it were and Mama got in touch with them. She asked Mr. Jimmy and his wife, Miss Havelon, who owned and ran the place, to write me a letter about how great it was so that I could be convinced to give camp another try. I still remember the green camp stationery and the typewritten letter addressed to *me*!

I stayed home the following summer but agreed to go when I was eleven. I was miserable again. This time, though, I stuck it out for a week, and that was long enough to get over the homesickness and start enjoying the place. The rest of the month turned out to be absolutely wonderful. Mr. Jimmy and Miss Havelon—their last name was Gearish—were high school teachers, teaching speech and music, respectively. They had become traveling entertainers and had fallen in love with the people and the hills of Middle Tennessee, bought some land, and opened a camp for kids. The buildings, deep in the woods, were hand-laid mountain stone. In the middle was a cast iron bell that clanged when it was time for meals or for activities that included swimming, archery, gunnery, tennis, badminton, and crafts. There was an old weathered barn, a softball field, a clay tennis court, a rifle range, and an outhouse we called "the library." The food was great. The Gearishes never had children of their own, but for four weeks every summer for boys, and another four for girls, they had dozens.

Miss Havelon was very pretty and had a beautiful voice, and I developed a big crush on her. At the worship service one Sunday morning, she sang a song that really moved me. It was called "Others" by Charles D. Meigs, and the second verse and chorus really spoke to me:

Help me in all the work I do
To ever be sincere and true
And know that all I do for you
Must needs be done for—Others.

Others, Lord, yes, others,
Let this my motto be
Help me to live for others
That I may live like thee.

All of my upbringing in Scottsville was there in that song's words: How well you live your life is largely determined by your attitude toward other people. If you truly care about them, you can mature beyond selfishness and really make your mark where it counts.

I wound up loving the place, and when I went back the following year, Mr. Jimmy asked me to talk to the other boys who were homesick.

While I was at camp, my mother sent regular letters, which were always newsy and fun. I felt wonderful about opening them until I received one that started out innocently enough, talking about a business trip she was taking with my father. Then she said trips always caused her to think about the possibility that she might not come back, and when she and Dad traveled together, she worried even more. She wondered what would happen if they were involved in a bad accident and did not return to their children!

After laying that particularly morbid thought on me, Mama reminded me that I was the oldest boy and therefore had a special responsibility in the event of their deaths, especially when it came to the baby of the family—my brother, Steve, who was then about five. More than anything, she said, she wanted him to be reared in a way that would give him the best chance at a happy and fulfilling life. But instead of a whole laundry list of dos and don'ts, Mama mentioned only one thing. "Please do all within your power to see that your brother understands the principles of fair play," she wrote.

Now, what on earth is a twelve-year-old kid supposed to do with that piece of advice?

That letter and her request would haunt me to some extent all my life. They led me to try to formulate some basic life principles, a quest that has interested me ever since. I think she wanted the concept of "fair play" to have broad application, and I came to see the principles behind it as believing in the dignity of all work, having a sense of humor, and developing a personal mission. They were all components of moral integrity, and if there's one precept I carried from what my parents and my faith taught me, it is that if you have a commitment to moral integrity, you don't need a bunch of picky rules. They aren't necessary; in fact, they become just so much unnecessary baggage. I think that's part of the core of what Jesus said, and all of this fit beautifully into my understanding of Christianity.

My mother wasn't worried so much about the precepts themselves as she was about someone bringing them to life for my brother. She wanted me to be the kind of person who exemplified them. It was the beginning of a lifelong desire to try to do just that.

Much of that side of my personality came from my mother, who oversaw a lot of my moral development. She was there with more practical advice as well, including some I thought would fall more naturally to my father.

"Son," she said once, "let me teach you how to fight. There are three rules. Rule number one is, don't ever get into a fight. You're smart enough to talk your way out of any situation that's leading in that direction, so there's no reason to get into a fight in the first place. Number two, if you *do* get into a fight, *don't lose.* When you decide to hit someone, hit him hard. If that doesn't work, pick up a stick and hit him, and if that doesn't work, pick up a rock. Don't lose. And rule number three—remember, don't ever get into a fight!"

Then there was the time we took a rare family vacation. I was eleven or twelve and we had gone to Daytona Beach and my mother asked me to take a walk with her. I couldn't understand why she was so nervous and tentative, but as we walked along the beach, she began talking about Laura Jo, explaining to me that she was having her first menstrual cycle. She stumbled through a talk about how this happens when a girl becomes a woman and how it's a thirty-day cycle related to how women have babies. I don't know if I caught everything she was saying, but I do remember how concerned I was about the extraordinary difficulty she was having with the conversation. I remember trying to help it along as much as I could.

My dad wasn't much on moral or spiritual instruction, and after working six days a week, he was much more attracted to the golf course than to church. What I got from my dad was a sense of camaraderie and companionship, although golf didn't really help foster that. I tried being a caddy, but it was work—hot work at that—and I didn't take to the game. To this day, I'm not very good at it.

Temperamentally, my father and I were very similar, but there were many day-to-day differences in our talents and interests. Some things he did well, I didn't, and vice versa. He was a great basketball player; I wasn't worth much out on the court. If somebody else wanted the ball that much more than I did, I thought he ought to have it. The competition of sports was never a big thing with me. When it became obvious my heart wasn't in basketball, my dad said, "Son, give it up," and that's what I did. I became the team statistician—and began working in the warehouse after school. Saturdays I'd work at our local retail store, Allen Dry Goods.

3

ᐧᕫᕮᐧ

Business: The Key
Turner Dynamic

Business was the backdrop for pretty much every family activity, sometimes even prayer. I remember Mama asking my sisters and me to pray for snow because my dad was overstocked on four-buckle overshoes—which, of course, he had overbought. Then one Christmas season, she asked us to pray for the snow to melt so customers could get to our stores. If they couldn't shop, he wouldn't be able to pay the bank at the end of the year. We learned at an early age that retailers desperately needed God's cooperation when it came to the weather. We also learned the importance of December, when Christmas shopping could make all the difference between staying in business another year and going under.

"In retailing," my grandfather used to say, "you lose money for eleven months, just hoping to make it all back in December. Then in January, you begin the struggle all over again!"

We also prayed for my dad. Mama made sure we asked God to help him not to work too hard. For all the lightheartedness in her personality, she, like many of our friends, worried sometimes that work might get the best of him. She had lost her own father when she was eighteen, so her worry tugged at a very deep loss. Later, his doctors would worry about my dad, too, but none of that affected him. Work was his life. It fed his spirit.

The hub of that work was the two-story brick warehouse on East Main Street. My dad would ship merchandise to the stores during the week from inventory reflecting his seemingly whimsical buying escapades, and he'd call them on Saturday night to see how they were doing.

Those calls were part of his routine until the 1960s. He called every store manager in the chain from an upstairs bedroom. The local operator, Miss Molly Pace, stayed one call ahead of him, telling the next store manager on the list that Mr. Turner would be with him in fifteen minutes. Every manager had to stay on Saturday night until he called. It was that important. It was a big deal to Miss Molly, too—the highlight of her week, as far as I could tell. I do believe she lived for the moments when my dad would brag about her for her help in connecting him to all those store managers.

"How much have we sold?" my dad asked those managers. "How much were the bank deposits?"

Retailing the Cal Turner way involved clean, friendly, high-performing stores, and Saturday night was when he got the chance to see that performance on paper. It was personal and it was all-consuming. He was always stretched perilously thin on cash, and he had to know precisely how much money would be flowing into Farmers National Bank in Scottsville from all those stores before the checks he'd written, mostly to vendors from whom he'd bought merchandise, were presented for payment Wednesday. He was, in short, playing the float. He was very good at it, and when he knew he couldn't cover his checks, he would get in the car with Luther and drive to Nashville to borrow some more money from Sam Flemming, who in 1950 had become president of Third National Bank.

Eventually, Sam urged my dad to buy into Farmers National Bank, and he loaned him the money to do so. My dad and my uncle Frank, Mama's brother, were both on the board, and while they sometimes fought like cats and dogs—Turners and Goads often looked at things differently—it was a great bit of synergy for my dad, who was on the board of an institution integral to his retail business, and for Sam and Third National, who now had another good correspondent bank—a business ally.

My dad had a great connection to the retailers in the small towns served by the stores because he was a small-town person himself. His love of his customers was definitely part of his approach to business as well. He respected them. He knew their families came from the same stock as he. They struggled; they got by with little.

"We've always identified the folks in small towns as those who could recognize the real value of merchandise," he said.

Only two or three of the stores bore the Turner name back then—Turner's Department Store in Horse Cave, Kentucky, was one—but they were all part of J. L. Turner and Son, and he kept a close eye on all of them. I'd visit stores with him occasionally, and as I got older, I watched more closely. He had incredibly high standards. He wanted a store to be clean and well displayed. He didn't want to see anything in the stockroom—it might as well have been buried. Every bit of merchandise should be available to the customer. He had opinions on the right way to do almost everything, and he never just told people. He always showed them. His training style was "energetic hands-on."

On the other hand, he thought the hard work of "keeping store" shouldn't harm the atmosphere for shoppers. He had a great personality with customers. He wasn't much with jokes or small talk, but he greeted everyone who walked through the door—and he liked the door to be wide open. He liked people and sincerely wanted them to feel welcome. He was happy to answer questions or help them find something. Like his father, he was a real Southern gentleman. He tipped his hat to the ladies and always held doors open for them.

Like my grandfather, my dad always dressed like a businessman, although he was more colorful. Whether he was in his warehouse office or on the road visiting stores, he wore a coat and tie. Especially early on, my mother might get a rose from her garden and pin it to his lapel as he left the house in the morning.

He was a no-nonsense boss, someone who expected everyone around him to work as hard as he did. In the warehouse, when it came time to get down to business, he'd take off his jacket, loosen his tie, undo the top button of his shirt, and roll up his sleeves. He thought of employees as family and was generally pleasant and enjoyable to be around. He and Luther threw a Christmas party for the office and warehouse employees in the early years, handing out a bonus and a box of candy to each. He and Mama also threw a dinner party for all the store managers and their wives at the Jacksonian Hotel in Scottsville to thank them for their partnership and the success they shared. One year, when my brother, Steve, was just five or so, my dad gave him a box of cigars to pass out to those attending. Steve came back after a while with a pile of bills in the box—he'd been selling them rather than giving them away! My dad said, "We have the makings of a great little merchant here." It was family, it was fun, and it was working. But my dad was always restless, always thinking. These were junior department stores, miniature versions of the bigger stores in Nashville and Louisville. He studied what the merchants there were doing and thought about ways to get even bigger.

Meanwhile, I studied my parents. Like most kids, I learned far more from them when they didn't know they were teaching. Fortunately, the biggest lessons from both were positive. I remember my mother saying, "Son, for a good boy, you get into a lot of trouble." That little statement provided a beautifully healthy separation of the person and the teenage crime. It said I was good even though my actions sometimes weren't. She helped me see the gap between who

I was and what I did, and reminded me there was an ideal to reach for. For the rest of my life, her approach positioned me to retain a sense of humor in the face of my own shortcomings and to try for a healthy ego management so I could better grasp the lessons I needed to learn.

Then there was the unstinting support and admiration I received from my father. My first job was sweeping the floor in the warehouse after school—I was thirteen or so and made 25 cents an hour. My dad made a point of coming into an aisle I'd just swept. He'd bring associates and say, "Look at this! Have you ever seen a floor that was swept as well as this?" He'd speak as if he didn't know I was within earshot as I swept the next aisle. And it worked. The more he bragged, the harder I swept.

That kind of approval is so important, since a parent's support can make all the difference in the world. I learned later of the parallels between the son of the founder of another chain of stores and me. He was better looking and more intelligent, he was a lawyer and a CPA, but he never really got the blessing the way I did. His father would get all over him if he came home with one B on a report card that otherwise had all A's. When I came home with the same report card, my dad would say, "Son, that's wonderful! I never thought a Turner could make grades this good." It was a great feeling. Dollar General became many times more successful than that chain, something I attribute largely to the influence of the founding fathers of each business and how they reared their sons. So much of success and failure lies in what we take from our primary relationships.

It was fun being part of the company that young, and I remember the kick Troy Connor, who drove for Wehby Trucking out of Nashville, got out of me. He called me "Little Tunna" as we unloaded cases and he counted each one. It was incredible to him that, at twelve or thirteen, I was working there.

It was fun and exciting, sometimes because it was such a seat-of-the-pants operation. There was no rhyme or reason when it came to the main warehouse and there still wasn't a loading dock; trucks just backed up to the front porch. After we'd stacked and counted the boxes on the porch, we'd take them in and store them wherever we could find space, which was always at a premium. Ideally, we'd unload them onto low tables or shelves, but usually there was so much merchandise coming in that a lot of it would simply be piled in the aisles. There just wasn't time to get it out and displayed in some sort of organized way. Finding anything was a nightmare.

Store managers came in once a week to see what the boss had bought lately and to pick out what they thought they needed. They'd load everything into a big cart and take it by Marie Foster's desk. Another worker would call off the items and Marie would type an invoice and give it to the manager as he left.

We'd cram their cars full of as much merchandise as we could, and the managers had invariably taken the backseats out so they'd hold even more. We'd take everything out of the boxes—shoes, shirts, blouses—and pack it loose in the trunk until we could barely get the lid down. Then we'd pack more into the rear, where the backseat had been, until it was jammed against the roof. If the manager had driven by himself, we'd fill the passenger seat too. If there was no mirror on the outside, we'd leave a hole right down the middle so he could see out the back in the rearview. It had to be a mess when they arrived at the stores, but our system allowed us to get the most goods possible into a very small space. Empty space, I learned then, is very expensive to haul around. I also learned how to pack a car— my wife, Margaret, is still impressed.

I learned priceless lessons working for the company in those years. It wasn't always fun, but it was educational—and it was a way of staying out of mischief after school and in the summer. About a year after I started, I got a raise to 35 cents an hour, and that's where it seemed to stay for the longest time. I always kept up with my own hours, and at one point Daddy hadn't paid me in a while. It got up to fifty or sixty hours. I really wanted that money. It wasn't that I was going to rush out and spend it on something foolish. I was a saver—I had been since the time when I found a lot of coins in the recliner we had given to my dad—and I enjoyed knowing I had money socked away. In fact, the rest of the family used to joke about the fact that when we were out somewhere and we needed or wanted something, I'd always tell them I had left my money at home.

So here I was anticipating this hard-earned windfall. I remember talking to Howard Cole about it, and he and I conspired to do something. We went to my dad.

"Mr. Turner," he said, "how much are we paying Cal Jr. per hour?"

I can still remember my dad saying, "Well, Howard, what do you think about minimum wage?" That was $1 an hour, nearly three times what I thought I was making. It was fabulous!

Howard helped me fill out a statement with a Dun & Bradstreet seal on it that listed the hours I'd worked, so it looked really official. Daddy got a kick out of that and he had someone go into the petty cash fund and take the money out. It was as much money as I'd ever seen.

My dad loved deal making, and he had his own style. In the early days, he, like many wholesalers and retailers in Kentucky and Tennessee, met with salesmen from New York in Nashville. One, named Harry Weiner, would meet with my dad at Nashville's Andrew Jackson Hotel. Early on, as Harry displayed his samples, my dad would say, much to Harry's amusement, "I'd like a hundred dollars' worth of Sunday-go-to-meeting dresses and a hundred dollars' worth of honeymoon gowns." The two quickly became good friends. My dad went to New York a few times a year to see what the clothing merchants had to offer, staying at the Statler Hotel near Penn Station at Seventh Avenue and 34th Street, so he had easy access to the Garment District.

He loved negotiating, enjoying the gamesmanship of it all. "It's just plain fun," he would say. It was obvious the sellers enjoyed it too. There was such a contrast between the negotiating styles of these flamboyant, fast-talking New Yorkers and this easygoing Southerner. Their deliberations were invariably about apparel. With brooms and detergent and toilet paper, volume determined the price. Clothing was a higher-ticket item with a greater markup potential, and so there was a great opportunity for wheeling and dealing, something Daddy loved. Along those lines, he knew what he had to have seasonally—school clothes, winter wear, Easter dresses, summer outfits—and he knew what his competitors were buying, so he was always responding to those forces. The salesmen would exaggerate the merits of the garments they were selling, and my dad would agree with them in his aw-shucks kind of way, then say, "Well, given my customers, this is all I can really spend on this."

Paul Polizzi, a manufacturer's representative who worked with my dad for forty years, said later, "He was an outstanding negotiator, but a fair negotiator. He knew the perceived value of a product, and what his customers needed and wanted. When he saw a good buy, he jumped right into it."

He started from a great position because they knew he paid his bills on time. That helped him get good prices. He was great at working the terms too. If they offered a 2 percent discount for paying within ten days, he'd pay then. If they didn't, he might negotiate for sixty days or ninety rather than thirty. He was also someone who never sent anything back. If you sold it to him, it stayed sold, whether or not he could sell it back home, so if they had a lot of a particular item or line at the end of a season, they'd give him a really good deal. He didn't normally believe in buying high-style clothing that was subject to volatile trends and might have to be closed out at the end of the season. He would rather buy items he could pack away and bring out the next season.

If those sellers wanted to get rid of something, they'd get in touch with my dad. It was fun for him to negotiate in his "You name the quantity, I'll name the price" style. He'd say, "I'll take all you've got. This is what I'm willing to pay." He was always proud of those deals.

Eventually, as the company grew, he didn't need to go to New York as often. Factory reps came to him. Still, he enjoyed going and playing the game in that world.

My dad took Mama with him most of the time, and now and then he'd take us kids. I remember our first trip, and how impressive the fast pace and tall buildings were to me. We visited Harry and Gladys Weiner, who lived at 55 Central Park West, and they took my parents, Laura Jo, and me—we were fifteen and thirteen, respectively—to the Latin Quarter to see Johnnie Ray, a flamboyantly emotional singer known for the hit "Cry."

We walked up to the maître d', who asked, "Do you have a reservation?" Harry said, "No, but see what you can do," flashing a twenty, which widened my eyes considerably. The maître d' took it with a deft and practiced grab and escorted us to a front-row table. Laura Jo was absolutely smitten with Johnnie Ray, and she was enthralled as he performed. At one point, he came off the stage and into the audience. He walked to our table, leaned down, and kissed Laura Jo—and she fainted. Then there was some sort of contest and I got up onstage. They made fun of my accent, but I had fun and the evening was a great one. We also saw Gwen Verdon in *Damn Yankees*, which was very impressive as well.

We'd often go to shows and we ate out regularly—I remember the New York waiters' reaction when Mama ordered ketchup to go with her scrambled eggs at breakfast, something they'd never heard of.

Once, one of my dad's vendors got Mama a spot on one of her favorite game shows, *Top Dollar*, which aired from a studio in New York. All of Scottsville knew she was going to be on TV, and everybody tuned in. Mama had watched the show every day and was really good at it. Sure enough, she won two or three rounds, but I remember that her flat Southern accent for some reason sounded awful on network television. Then she was asked to identify a certain kind of sausage. The answer was "knockwurst" and she didn't get it. I can still hear her saying, "That's not fair! We don't have that in Scottsville!" Everybody roared and that was the round she lost. As the show went off the air, they brought out a "knockwurst necklace" and placed it around her neck, which really embarrassed me, although she was a good sport and enjoyed herself.

Not long after my first New York trip, in 1953, we moved into a big colonial-style home at 215 West Cherry Street. It had thick brick walls and stood on six acres right across from the jail, something we used to joke about. My dad paid $25,200 for it and then had to scramble for the cash to landscape and remodel it. My mother brought in an interior design firm, but my dad said they could only redo the two downstairs rooms in the front of the house—the living room and the den—because that was all we could afford.

The remodeling process was especially memorable because when they tore out one of the floors, they found a big tree stump beneath it. Apparently, the builders had cut the tree low enough that they could build over it and never bothered to take out the stump.

The landscape designer—a woman whose purple hose I still remember, as they made her legs look like big eggplants—took one look at the large, unimproved expanse of ground on which the house sat and waylaid my dad as he blew by on his way out the door. She said, "Congratulations, Mr. Turner. You have built a mansion on the city dump, but I can fix it." I'd never seen anyone so handily stop him in his tracks.

She did indeed fix it, and when the improvements had been made, we had a huge open house for the community. We brought in Luella Lambert and her Hammond organ so she could provide music. My parents invited the town's teetotalers for the first two hours and those who imbibed for the next two, spiking the punch in between. Even in a small town, knowing who fits into which category can be tricky, and my parents laughed at how many members of the early crowd stayed into the second portion of the evening and how much they seemed to enjoy themselves.

4

❧

"Every Day Is Dollar Day"

I was fifteen when my dad took the step that changed everything. It involved the kind of creative leap that comes along all too rarely, and it ultimately left a huge mark on American business.

We had thirty-six stores in small Kentucky and Tennessee towns grossing about $2 million annually, and my dad was always looking for ways to grow. He was a keen observer of both his customers and the competition, and he became intrigued by the "Dollar Days" sales put on by the big department stores in Nashville and Louisville. Once a month, they would take out huge full-color newspaper ads and sell merchandise with $1 as the single price point. My dad knew what those ads cost, and he understood that if they were spending that kind of money, they were selling a lot of goods. Customers obviously loved that $1 price point. Somehow, it made real value seem even more obvious.

Why couldn't we simplify all of our operations, he thought, *by opening a store with only one price—a dollar?* Every *day would be Dollar Day*. In that flash of insight, he saw any number of benefits. Customers could keep track of what they were spending more easily, and checkout would be simplified.

My dad was convinced he had something. He walked into work the next day and asked his management team to join him in his office. He told them he wanted to sell everything in every store for

$1. In some cases it would be multiples, like three plates or two pairs of socks for $1, but nothing would cost more.

"What do you think?" he said.

"Cal," they told him, "it'll never work. You can't buy enough merchandise to sell that cheap!" They were especially concerned about apparel, since so much of it sold for more than $1. But Cal Turner, Sr., was the classic entrepreneur—he followed his gut, and his gut told him this would work. He trusted his knowledge of customers more than he trusted the opinions of even those closest to him. He decided to do it.

He would start with a store that had failed. It was in Springfield, Kentucky, and it had operated at a loss as a junior department store. It would provide a great test of whether this new concept would work.

That left choosing a name. The word *Dollar* was a must—that was the whole point. With a nod to the term *general store*, he added the word *General*. He was an opportunity buyer. He looked for bargains, and the word *General* would let customers know they might find just about anything inside. He often said, "Back in the country, the general store is where everything and anything was sold." The *Dollar General* sign, he decided, would be black and yellow, a combination he knew really stood out.

"I wanted the colors to leap right off the store signs," he said.

The opening was set for Wednesday, June 1, 1955. Turner's Department Store on Main Street in Springfield would become the first Dollar General store. The layout was clean and simple, with big bold red $1 signs seemingly everywhere. Its slogan was "Every Day Is Dollar Day."

On the big day, people crowded around the front of the building by the hundreds. The manager knew he wouldn't be able to let them all in at once, so when he opened, he let customers in until the place was good and crowded and then shut the doors behind them. As they came out, he let new people in. He and my father had a hit on their hands, and my dad had a concept he could take to other stores in the chain—where the scenario of huge crowds at grand openings would be repeated over and over.

The second store was in Memphis. Dad bought the Goodwin Crockery Company, a wholesaler with an office and a big warehouse on Union Street. It wasn't exactly a prime retail market; there were used car lots here and there and not much else. Dad loaded the building with merchandise and opened for business. Selling nothing for more than $1, that store had sales of $1.1 million in the first ten months—"a million, one hundred and thirteen thousand dollars," my dad said to me. "Isn't that amazing!" Dad knew he had something.

He opened and converted other stores, eager to reproduce that early success and always looking for the next opportunity. My dad knew he was changing the customers' entire way of thinking. This was a different way to present value, avoiding common price points like 49 cents, which would now be two for $1. In his stores, they wouldn't be looking at a host of individual prices anymore. They'd be thinking, *Look what I can get for a dollar. I can get ten of these forks or four of these saucers, and since I can mix and match, I can get five forks and two saucers for a dollar.*

He was changing the approach of his buyers as well. He had always worked with a few people who could deal with vendors and haggle over the prices for everything but the clothing he so loved dealing with, but my dad didn't believe in having a lot of buyers. For a long time, *he* had been the buyer, and gradually he'd been training people to do what he did. Still, it was a long, slow process for him to get to the point where he'd trust them to implement the decision making he'd honed through the years.

Classically, it had been, "I'll negotiate the best price I can, then add my thirty percent markup, and that will be the retail price." Now they'd have to think in terms of one price point—$1—and then common-sense multiples like two for $5, something that became clear after he'd priced shoes at $1 apiece to conform with his slogan—"Nothing over a dollar." Some people would buy just one! He wound up with mismatched shoes, so he went to $2 per pair of shoes, and other multiples of $1 weren't far behind. The important thing was that each bill in a customer's pocket represented a unique and easily understood price point. He or she would know what each would buy.

Each price point would have to mark a clear step up in value. As a buyer bought for the upcoming Christmas season, he'd be thinking, *What is the best stocking stuffer we can offer a customer for a dollar? What kind of gift or toy can we price at five dollars?* Then, *What is going to be the one* big *toy for that child that we can offer at ten dollars?* You'd have crisp, differentiated levels of value in your store, and your customer could understand the system and keep up with what she was spending.

My dad knew it would require real discipline.

"With the dollar strategy, the discipline is forced on you," he said. "With virtually every item less than ten dollars and with the pricing at one-dollar breaks, there is not much room to stretch. Price-point retailing takes nerve, and we've had the nerve. We have to be better merchants to operate in this niche. We have to 'cream the lines' we carry to have the greatest possible offering in a small store. We have to make every item count. We have to recognize that if we make a mistake, we've got to get it out of there quickly. I'm not one for false pride."

Dad knew there were times they'd have to sell below cost to give the best deals possible to the customers while sticking with that $1 price. If he was buying, for example, cold pack canners, big covered pots used in home canning, he might pay $12.75 a dozen. He knew they'd make great $1 items that would help bring in customers, so that's where he'd price them. On the other hand, he might be buying cheap ceramics from Japan at $5 a dozen. He'd price those at

$1 too. He wanted the store employees thinking they were making a profit on everything they sold, to keep them smiling through both sales, and he'd handle the markup at the wholesale level. He'd bill both items to the stores at $10 a dozen, and they'd sell them for $1 a piece, or $12 a dozen, a markup of $2 per dozen. Meanwhile, the warehouse was getting $20 from the store for items for which it paid a total of $17.75. The ceramics covered the loss they would have shown on the canners. That way, they wouldn't show a loss of $2.75 on every dozen cold pack canners. For good measure, it would mystify his competitors, who knew Dad was selling those canners for less than they were buying them wholesale, and wondered how he could possibly be getting such a good price.

Sometimes, he knew, he'd have to go to the vendor and say, "I can't pay you that much. I've got to sell this at a dollar. Can you work with me?" He would actually become an agent for the customer. It would take discipline and stubbornness, qualities Cal Sr. had in abundance.

One early episode epitomized the popularity of the store and the effectiveness of good pricing. My dad's friend Guy Comer, who owned Washington Manufacturing Company, was drowning in pink corduroy material at the end of a short-lived pink-and-black craze. Struggling to sell anything and everything he could for $1, my dad said, "Why don't you cut that up and make men's pants that I can sell for a dollar?"

Mr. Comer wasn't able to do it quite that cheaply, but he came close enough that Daddy bought a lot of them at far less than he'd have to pay for other pants of that quality. There was nothing else Mr. Comer could do with the material, so he went along. My dad would be selling them at a loss, but they'd bring people in the store. He sold them at $1 a pair—50 cents a leg—and his customers were practical enough that, regardless of the gaudy pink color, they recognized value and bought them, and although it was summer, they wore them. Through the years, people have told stories about visitors to Springfield being confronted that summer with downtown streets that had a decidedly pink hue!

In 1955, my dad and grandfather incorporated the business, which included thirty-six stores in partnership with local merchants. These were self-service stores, as opposed to the old general store, where the proprietor would gather the things you wanted, or the department store, where a clerk helped you with your purchase. Self-service opened the whole store to the customer. There was a price on every item and you helped yourself. The cash register was near the front door. The stores carried wearing apparel, shoes, domestics (things like towels and pillowcases), and household items of every sort.

The number of stores stood at twenty-nine in 1957, as a few of the less-successful ones had closed and partners had bought Dad out in others, but sales had more than doubled to $5 million. Small-town merchants began coming to Scottsville, seeking to become part of Dollar General. My dad never sought out franchisees, but he welcomed those who came. He also hand-picked some people to work with. He offered a man named Glenn Garrison a job as a store manager in Horse Cave, Kentucky. Glenn said he didn't know anything about running a store.

"Glenn," my dad said, "if you knew anything about running a store, I wouldn't want you. I want to train you myself."

At about the time my dad launched Dollar General, I encountered a man who would change my life, although I saw him only once and I wouldn't realize his impact until years later, when I was in college. I was working at Allen Dry Goods, the family store on the square in Scottsville. I wasn't any good at store work—to this day, I can't find anything—so I had the customers nobody else wanted, and I remember as if it were yesterday trying to make a sale to a farmer struggling over the purchase of a 39-cent pair of panties (here we are with pant-ies again!) for his wife.

He was an older man, with dirty, worn overalls and work shoes, big ears, a face full of stubble, and ambeer-stained cheeks. He smelled like tobacco and old sweat.

"I need to buy panties for the old lady," he said.

"What size does she wear?" I asked him.

"I don't know."

Great, I thought. *This is going to take forever, and when it's all said and done, I will only have made a thirty-nine-cent sale.*

"Well, we have to know the size," I said. "How big is she?"

He pointed to my aunt Ethel, who worked in the store.

"She's about her size."

Now we're getting somewhere! I thought.

Aunt Ethel was our best clerk, and at the moment she was waiting on a customer. She had a big armful of merchandise she was about to ring up.

"Ethel!" I yelled, in a voice that boomed across the crowded store. "What size panties do you wear?" Well, she made a noise like a gobbling turkey, threw the merchandise in the air, and went run-ning, red-faced, to the stockroom. I walked over and finished her sale, then went back to the farmer. Seeing that Ethel wasn't going to cooperate, we just held the panties up to look at them and he tried to imagine whether or not they'd fit.

As we talked, I realized that he didn't want to be in that discus-sion any more than I did. He was there because his wife had asked him to come. He was making a sacrifice for the "old lady," and he needed me to help so he could get out of there. I understood in that moment that we were connected.

Then I realized that the sacrifice wasn't just his time or any embarrassment he felt. He had to do this right because 39 cents was a meaningful amount of money. To him, every penny that came in and went out meant something.

It occurred to me what vastly different lives we led. The Turners were so much better off than this poor old farmer, who was, like many of our customers, surely struggling just to get by. If there was anybody in that community who needed help, it was he and those like him. For the first time, I was looking right through the dirt and the tobacco juice and the smell and connecting with this customer. The Mr. Fix-It part of my personality had connected with the need this man had for value in everything he bought.

He reminded me a little of my grandfather, who started out as a poor dirt farmer, and who still embarrassed me somewhat with his unpolished English. But where Luther had harnessed his willingness to work toward a dream and had gotten off the farm, this man never would.

I usually felt like a misfit around our customers. They seemed crude and unsophisticated, like this old codger, and it wasn't until later that I realized the problem was simply my youthful, judgmental arrogance. What I did realize in that moment was that he was poor, and that since my life was so different, I must be rich.

I wondered if the "old lady" knew how much he loved her. Heck, I wondered if *he* knew how much he loved her, how sweet his willingness to sacrifice really was. And I doubt he ever had a clue as to the impact he had on me.

Meanwhile, Dollar General was growing. I could tell the concept was working, because the office and warehouse kept getting busier and busier. I watched the growth firsthand while working in our second warehouse, a converted tobacco barn outside town, and it wasn't long before other retailers recognized what a good idea Cal Turner had. Most impressive of all was still our Memphis store. Businessmen from all over the South, people who owned dime or variety stores, came to study it, and some visited Scottsville to talk to my dad about it—he didn't think he had any secrets and he would tell anyone who asked anything he wanted to know. Of course, he was astute enough that he got as much information out of those conversations as they did. The chains whose owners drew inspiration from that store included Fred's, owned by the Baddour family; the Main Dollar Store in Memphis; Top Dollar in Jasper, Alabama; and United Dollar out of Dumas, Arkansas.

Bill's Dollar Store in Columbia, Mississippi, got started when my dad lost his bid to buy a group of Yellow Front Stores to Bill Walker. Once Bill had bought the stores, he came to Scottsville to learn the dollar store business, bringing his buyers in to buy merchandise from J. L. Turner and Son. They would walk through the warehouse and write down the names of vendors so they could contact them and establish their own relationships with them.

No matter how admired and imitated my father was, our company was still a downhome operation. At first, we had just a big van and one truck, and then we moved up to having two tractors, four trailers, and a '55 Chevy pickup truck to transport merchandise. My dad, always as good at promotion as he was at selling, had *Dollar General Stores, "The Town's Most Unusual Store,"* painted in black and yellow the length and height of every truck in order for them to be "moving billboards." You couldn't miss them. He had it printed on the paper bags used in the stores as well. He was very proud, by the way, when he read that black and yellow was the most effective color combination in terms of visibility and punch!

I loaded and unloaded my share of those things in my teens. Often I worked with an African American fellow named John Starks. We called him J.L., or Jay, and he and I did a lot of real grunt work. I remember getting cocky one day as we were unloading trucks. At one point I decided to take the liberty of jumping into the cab of one of those rigs and backing it up to the loading dock. After all, I was sixteen and had my driver's license, and *somebody* had to do it. I was the boss's son, so no one stopped me. It was an intriguing process figuring out how to turn right to make the trailer go left and all the rest. Amazingly enough, I pulled it off, backing one up to the dock successfully. So then J.L. decided *he'd* do it. He got in and started backing it up and the big square back end of that thing took off a corner of the awning. That effectively ended our driving careers, even though, in a way, it had not been my fault. "There will be no more of that, Cal Jr.," was my dad's only comment.

Jay and I were buddies. We got a kick out of each other. His older brother, L.C., was the first employee my grandfather ever had. Scottsville had a small African American population, and I was never aware of racial friction. The struggling economy of Scottsville needed as much of everybody's money, black and white, as it could get.

Just as the town had a generally congenial atmosphere, Dollar General, for all its early growth, felt like a small company. I remember a party for store managers when I was sixteen. It was the night the first Turner grandchild—my older sister's first child—was born. The birth came early and my mother, as hostess of the "store party," couldn't make it to Louisiana. She was "fit to be tied" that she was home, missing an event this momentous, but she went ahead and hosted the dinner party.

Every year, someone would ask her to sing and she never would— until that year. It may have been that she was feeling the blues that night, because she honored the request. "Please, Laura, sing the 'St. Louis Blues,'" someone said. Luella Lambert was at the piano, and though they hadn't practiced, Mama got up and sang. I remember being embarrassed at how much emotion she put into it. You could see that song written all over her face.

As the Dollar General concept took off in the late 1950s, my grandfather spent less time with the business and more and more on his farm. He recognized that he was losing mental function and knew it would only get worse. He gave my dad power of attorney and began gifting his company stock to family members, planning his estate so that we wouldn't be faced with heavy taxes when he died.

I still remember the vacant stare in his eyes just before he was sent to the Seventh-Day Adventist Hospital in Madison, Tennessee, for shock treatments. I had the greatest respect and love for Papa, and watching him endure this terrible procedure was gut wrenching.

I remained sensitive when it came to things like that, and I sought solace in the Methodism that channeled the spiritual awakening I'd felt at eleven. The time I spent in and around church was at least equal to the time I spent in extracurricular activities at school. I was part of almost everything that went on and a prominent part of much of it. I was church organist and a regular at Sunday school and Methodist Youth Fellowship meetings.

Church was a natural venue for me. I could feel an inner thirst being at least partially quenched there. It also felt good to get the approval of the little old ladies, who were prone to saying things like, "Cal Jr., I'm praying that you're going to be a preacher." I could gauge their sincerity by the fact that they sometimes had tears rolling down their cheeks.

Church also fed my intellectual development, as I thought through the doctrinal differences of the various denominations. Some thought other denominations were going to hell. *Who is right?* is a question I had to think through.

Then there was the hypothetical scenario that went like this: Suppose you were saved but died before you were actually baptized? Some, because of their literal interpretation of Peter's "Confess Christ and be baptized" as the full prescription, said you would go to hell. Of course, there are other places in the New Testament that say if you believe in Jesus, you're saved, but this one goes a step further. If nothing else, reasoning and arguing with friends—youth is a great time for that—helped me realize I'm a pretty good Methodist. I knew that John Wesley, speaking of doctrine, had said, "Let all these smaller points stand aside. Let them never come into sight. If your heart is as my heart, if you love God and all mankind, I ask no more: give me your hand." That sat well with me. It's not the denomination. It's not the belief. It's the relationship.

There was something much bigger that tugged at me underneath that argument. I realized that if it hadn't been for one small event, I'd have been a Baptist instead of a Methodist. The Turners were all Baptists and so were the Goads, but my mother and her brother Frank, who was a year older and whom she idolized, went to a Methodist revival as teenagers. She often did what he did, so when he walked down the aisle and joined the church, she followed him, and the two Baptists who walked into the revival came home Methodists.

My spiritual outlook figured prominently in my early thoughts about what I wanted to do with my life. Being surrounded from birth by the family business didn't mean I knew it would become my career. In fact, I felt called to ministry based on my experience of Jesus Christ on that Sunday evening when I was eleven, and on a further conversion experience at a Billy Graham crusade in Nashville a couple of years later. John Wesley described my experience best when he said in discussing his Aldersgate conversion that his heart felt "strangely warmed." That warmth, that experience of the presence of God, has always had a claim on me and has always motivated me. I knew my life would be a response to that claim, although I wasn't sure at that point which direction it would take.

I thought for a time about being a doctor, and when I brought it up, my dad knew just what to do. He talked to our family physician, Dr. Owen L. Davis, who arranged for me to take off from school to witness an operation. He'd be operating on a man's stomach, he told me. I thought he and Daddy were doing me a favor, helping me get a jump-start on my dream. I didn't realize until years later that it was a conspiracy to do just the opposite.

I met him at Allen County Memorial Hospital, scrubbed up with him, got in a gown, and accompanied him to the operating room. It wasn't long before I discovered he hadn't been altogether truthful. As I stood there looking over his shoulder, Dr. Davis removed a man's very enlarged testicle. I can still remember a nurse carrying it around the operating room to the amusement of everyone but me, looking for the container that would carry it to Vanderbilt University Hospital for testing.

I went back to school the next day and the secretary stopped me.

"What was the operation you saw, Cal?"

"I don't want to talk about it," I said.

I graduated from Scottsville High School in 1958 as valedictorian, which simply meant I made better grades than the twenty-six others in the class. I had been visualizing college as an opportunity to take a much-needed break from Scottsville and my family. As much as I loved them both, I wanted to step out of the shadows they cast on me and discover who I was.

One day as I looked through a stack of college brochures, picturing life on a campus thousands of miles from home, my dad walked over and picked one up.

"Son," he said, "I admire a man who makes up his own mind, and I want you to go to school anywhere you want. But I'll pay your way to Vanderbilt."

Well, I thought, *it might be good to get their catalog!*

I enrolled at Vanderbilt the next fall, eventually aiming for a BA in business administration with a minor in philosophy and political theory. I chose the minor in consultation with the divinity school so that if I changed my mind, I would be reasonably qualified to pursue training there.

The call to ministry remained strong, yet it was not something I welcomed. In fact, it scared the heck out of me. Still, there was no setting it aside completely.

My dad had known how to persuade me out of medicine, but he didn't know how to dissuade me from the ministry. It took a preacher to do that. Methodist churches swapped out preachers every four years or so, and Scottsville Methodist had just done that. I was a sophomore at Vanderbilt when I had my first encounter with Brother Woodson on a trip home.

"I understand you're considering the ministry," he said.

"Yes, sir, I am."

"Well, here's my advice. Don't do it."

I was shocked.

"I'm serious," he said. "Find anything else you can do and do that, because only if there's nothing else you can do are you truly called to be a preacher of the gospel of Jesus Christ. There are far too many preachers who were never called in the first place."

As the shock wore off, I found that I was actually relieved. There was a lot about being a preacher I didn't want—the little old ladies swooning over me, people pretending to listen every Sunday, and all the politics and bureaucracy that go with running a church. But that meant I had to dig deeper into myself. *What does God want for me?* I thought. There was a parallel question. *What is life's greatest challenge?*

Then it came to me.

Oh, heck, I thought. *I've got to go into the family business!* I recoiled at first because it meant I would not get to become my own person. But then I pictured my dad holding on to the company forever and running it into the ground because, it seemed, there was no one he'd trust it with besides me. I was Cal Jr.—I would have to be the boss's son, learn the business, and eventually take over.

In the wake of that discussion with Brother Woodson, I knew deep down where I was really headed. I came to realize that maybe I could have much more effect on the lives of our customers day in and day out in our stores than I ever could as a preacher conducting three services a week. *Maybe*, I thought, *I have a greater calling here.*

Maybe I had found something that was, for me, bigger and more fitting. In fact, I finally realized that life's greatest challenge would be to accept the subservience of ego necessary to go into business as the boss's son, rather than be "my own man."

I thought back to that ambeer-stained farmer buying the 39-cent panties and to the hundreds of people like him who came in and out of our stores. I realized pretty quickly that they were a lot smarter than I in many ways. They knew things about life and work that I didn't. They were worldly-wise customers who didn't quite trust a cocky young whippersnapper sales boy. They were especially smart about determining real value as opposed to perceived value. They couldn't be fooled by displays or packaging. You couldn't tempt them with sale items they didn't need. They walked by everything except what they had come in for, and if you didn't have it, they would simply walk back out.

They prompted me to look at the everyday dynamics of the business differently. I had always heard my dad and grandfather agree that low-end retailing is the struggling, gutsy end of the business. You have to work the dickens out of your people and you can't pay them much in order to keep your overhead low and survive, because, as I heard my father say so many times, "All I expect my competition to do to me is…everything he can do!"

Why couldn't a company like ours recruit people who could be motivated to have an impact on those who, like that farmer, really needed a better life? I thought, *Wait a minute! What if we could recruit from our customer base?* I believe God paints with a broad brush when it comes to creativity, and that it sometimes comes in unlikely packages. They would understand our customers because they *were* our customers. They could be excited about sharing the business with us. Retailing is a people-centered business anyway, and if people are motivated, they actually work harder than if a boss yells at them to work hard. We could work to give value to the customers and still reward employees. It would be a way to affect lives, financially and otherwise, day in and day out. Maybe I really had been called into this business.

Although I hadn't been good at all at my early retail experience, I had been profoundly affected by that episode with the old farmer. It was the start of a lifetime in the family business, a lifetime of trying to serve people. It turned out I *was* called into true ministry— ministry that matters in the real world, the world of hurt and pain and error and sin, which to my mind was an even higher calling than the institutional ministry. It was a call that would be the central dynamic of my life.

5

Academic and Leadership Testing: Vanderbilt and the Navy

I enjoyed college; it was exciting and I felt challenged. I lived with a roommate in Barnard Hall, a freshman dorm, and then had a private room in Branscomb Quadrangle for the next three years. I joined Beta Theta Pi, but knew better than to live in the house. I wanted to be able to study when I wanted and sleep when I wanted, and I knew that living in a frat house wouldn't necessarily be conducive to either.

I was in Vanderbilt's School of Arts and Sciences, working toward a BA in business administration. At one point, I needed to improve my grade in freshman English and the assignment at hand was a paper on a poem. Our instructor, a graduate student named Mr. Lott, had read and poked fun at Joyce Kilmer's "Trees." As he was doing that, I remember thinking, *I agree with Kilmer, not you.* I loved the poem and felt almost personally attacked when he went after it. My assignment was to critique some obscure poem that I didn't think I understood, but I sequestered myself in my dorm room and thought, *Okay, Cal, what's the most outlandish stuff you can sling here? Push yourself! Come up with something zany.* I gave it the most esoteric and startling interpretation I could and apparently Mr. Lott bought what I was selling, because the result was an A.

I recall being very impressed with a management policies course that featured a lot of case studies under Professor David Steine, who was also a partner at J. C. Bradford, a major regional brokerage firm. Mr. Steine brought an urbane Southern gentility into the classroom. He called himself a businessman and respected us as future business management professionals. On the other hand, I was very unimpressed with a marketing course that seemed like a hodgepodge of packaging and advertising that didn't know what it wanted to be when it grew up.

Perhaps the most important course I took was managerial accounting, which taught me about the relationship between decisions and the numbers behind them. It took me beyond credits, debits, income statements, and balance sheets to demonstrate that you could re-sort your data to shed light on the decision you were trying to make in matters such as leasing versus purchasing or the desirability of outsourcing a given activity.

It also taught me, among other things, a healthy disdain for accounting. Consistency seemed to be the highest priority of accounting, and as Emerson told us, "A foolish consistency is the hobgoblin of little minds."

In 1962, when I was a senior at Vanderbilt, J. L. Turner and Son had seventy-six Dollar General stores, and my dad made the decision to go public. In fact, one session in my management policies class under David Steine that year was devoted to the prospectus of the initial public offering of our stock—Steine's company, J. C. Bradford, wanted participation in the deal. Then the market went south and my dad, advised that the stock would decline after the public offering, withdrew the offer rather than let his friends suffer a loss after buying the stock.

I graduated college in June 1962, the first member of my family to do so. Mama and Daddy were extremely proud of me, and their present to me was to pay for flying lessons, something I very much wanted to take. That summer, I drove twenty-five miles to and from

Bowling Green twice a day to take lessons. In a little over two months I had the hours I needed for my license, so I took the written exam and waited for the results.

I may have known where I was going with my life, but I was in no real hurry to get there. I still wanted time away from Scottsville, my dad, and the business. I wanted to learn about myself and my capabilities outside that goldfish bowl.

The more I thought about the next few years, the more the military made sense. I was eligible for the draft, and enlisting would give me some control over how I entered the service. I looked at the Navy. A college graduate could sign up for four months of training and be commissioned an ensign, a word I did not know how to pronounce at the time! It seemed a great way to learn leadership—at least the military's version of it.

So in August, I went to Newport, Rhode Island, to Naval Officer Candidate School. They were taking college graduates who knew nothing about the military and trying to break them down to see if they had what it took to become naval officers. They were going to have the seemingly impossible task of extracting the last ounce of ego from Cal Turner, Jr. I soon learned that they were willing to work on that with a great deal of dedication and enthusiasm.

I'll never forget my first night there. I checked in at the office and they told me how to get to my barracks. As I approached them with my duffel bag, some guys who had been there for two months were leaning out of windows, yelling, "Go home! It's hell!" The sun was setting, I'd been traveling all day, and I was exhausted. I flopped into the bottom rack of the bunk bed in the clothes I was wearing and went to sleep. Sometime during the middle of the night, I heard a fellow come in and climb into the upper rack.

They woke us before dawn and I sleepily introduced myself to the man in the upper bunk. He said his name was Paul Barra. Now, if you're from the South, "Paul Barra" is how you pronounce "pall bearer." I looked at him and said, "That's exactly what I need. A pall bearer."

Military life was certainly an adjustment for me. There were twenty-five of us in the head every morning, lined up at four sinks to shave or at the commodes or showers, yelling at the guys in front of us to hurry. You had to shave and shower, get your quarters ready for inspection, get in your uniform, and then march as a unit to the mess hall for breakfast. We marched everywhere, with one of us calling cadence and with John Philip Sousa music playing. I still associate Sousa with all the marching I did.

The school combined rigorous all-day class work—weapons and gunnery, navigation, seamanship, signaling—with all the elements of basic training, all crammed into four months.

I never looked forward to inspections, which happened right after breakfast. They always amounted to an officer, a lieutenant in this case, finding a bunch of Mickey Mouse infractions, or gigs. You could get them for unshined shoes, unpolished brass, or failing to have a straight gig line, the alignment of shirt buttons, belt, and fly. You could get them for all sorts of other things, including a missed spot shaving, and given the ratio of men to sinks and the fact that we were always rushed, missing a spot wasn't hard to do.

After afternoon class work and a brief break, we had dinner, then study hall. It made for an extremely long day. After study hall, right before bed, we got to take a break down at the vending machine, and I looked forward every day to the one real treat available there, an orange and vanilla Dreamsicle. I still remember how good it tasted.

The course work, especially combined with all the physical activity and those long days, was tough. I was starting from scratch on most everything, and *rigorous* doesn't begin to describe it. I had never been a hunter, and though I had shot at targets at Camp Dunroamin,

I wasn't skilled with or fond of guns, and of course I'd never been exposed to signaling with flags. Every class was a major challenge. It would have been difficult to place me in a more foreign world!

I had gone to a great university and taken a very intense course of study, but this was something else altogether. I consider Naval Officer Candidate School to be my first real brush with failure. At Vanderbilt, examinations mostly called for long essay answers. At the end of the semester, the professor would come up with a statement that formed the basis of the final exam, something that drew on everything learned in the course. In the Navy, there were multiple-choice examinations that started with the command "Pencils up!" and ended with "Pencils down." It was intense. Given the workload and the strangeness of the material, I almost flunked out. At one point I was called in by the company officer for the kind of chewing out officers have developed into an art form.

"I can't believe the kind of university they run down there in Nashville, Tennessee!" he said. "You graduated with honors and you can't pass your naval weapons course! I'm going to have to get in touch with them about their standards. They let somebody like *you* out with honors, you sorry son of a bitch!"

I was as frustrated as I'd ever been, down physically, emotionally, and probably spiritually. I stewed and stewed about it, and then one Sunday afternoon I went down to the cold, windblown Rhode Island shore. I couldn't cry, but as the waves crashed, I just started screaming into the wind. I yelled incoherently, in what amounted to this great wordless release, until it was all out of my system. I went back thinking, *You know, whatever it takes, I'm going to get through this. I am not going to flunk out of four months of Officer Candidate School and have to spend my time as an enlisted man. I'm just not going to do that.* I began to feel a lot more confident that I could do whatever I had to do.

At about that time, I received my private pilot's license in the mail. It was nice, after all the trouble I'd been having, to have that feeling of accomplishment, even though I had no intention of pursuing flying in the Navy.

The military still had its trials. It was tough to avoid the occasional gig at inspection, and if you got five, you lost your weekend privileges and had to stay on the base and march them off. Your roommate could cost you gigs as well, and I had a lanky lawyer named Phil Taliaferro, a fellow Kentuckian, sharing quarters with me. He never took anything very seriously and was really sloppy. I'd have to help him get shaped up so he'd pass inspection, and then I'd have to clean up *for* him so our *quarters* would pass inspection.

I remember getting my fifth red gig just before Veterans Day 1962, when I was scheduled to meet my parents in New York. Now I was going to have to stay on board and march all weekend. I told Phil about it and he said, "Got you covered." He was the political type, and he had landed a job as yeoman in our company officer's office, which meant he had access to the files. He went through the stack of paperwork for those who had to march off their red gigs, pulled mine, and brought it to me for my disposal. Fortunately, I'm a backsliding Methodist rather than a Baptist, so that was fine with me. I got to New York, had a great dinner with my parents Friday night, and didn't have to be back on base until Monday.

That Saturday morning, my dad got a call at the hotel saying there was a union organization effort going on among the employees in Scottsville. Some of them were signing cards asking for an election, an up or down vote on whether to be represented by the machinists' union. He got physically ill and stayed in the room all weekend while Mama and I enjoyed the city. When the trip was over, my dad went home and pulled out all the stops. He was ready for major warfare because he felt it was clearly so wrong for the company ever, ever, ever to have a union. He didn't want anyone telling him how to run his business. He wanted to determine whom to hire, what to pay them, and what their jobs were.

It was inevitable that he would react. For starters, as controlling stockholder of the largest bank in town, he was in a position to imply that loans might be a lot harder to come by if that union came in. That may have been illegal, and I'm not sure if Daddy knew whether it was or wasn't at the time, although if he had, I don't know that it would have mattered, he was so livid. In any case, the union effort failed.

At the end of my four months of training, in December 1962, I was commissioned Ensign, United States Naval Reserve, and after a quick Christmas break, I reported to the Naval Amphibious Base at Little Creek in Norfolk, Virginia. I went through orientation and reported to the USS *Pocono* (AGC-16). During my tour, it was the flagship for two commands—a rear admiral who was an amphibious task force commander, and the commander of Amphibious Forces, U.S. Atlantic Fleet, Vice Admiral John McCain, the father of senator and 2008 presidential candidate John McCain.

Admiral McCain was, to put it diplomatically, a stickler—*harsh, demanding perfectionist* is a little closer to the mark. He wanted everything done precisely by the book, which meant when he or any other dignitary boarded or left the ship, the side boys, who were sailors serving as an honor guard, had to look extra sharp, and all the piping, ruffles, and flourishes had to be just so. That's why all of us were so delighted by one particular episode. We got the word on deck that the admiral was coming on board and so everything came to a stop and everybody came to attention. Then, just as Admiral McCain reached the deck, a very slovenly sailor wandered out onto the pier with a load of garbage. He never stopped; he never even looked up. He just walked on by. Admiral McCain was furious.

"I want that sailor in my stateroom immediately," he said to the officer of the deck, and he stormed off to wait. The OOD got the attention of the sailor, who put down his garbage can and went up to the admiral's stateroom.

Admiral McCain went up one side of him and down the other for fifteen minutes or so, lecturing him at top volume about respect, rank, Navy decorum, and all the rest of it, using his normally salty approach. In fact, we called him "Goddammit McCain" because he couldn't get a sentence out that didn't call for the Deity's judgment. We worried when he *didn't* cuss. The sailor just kind of stood there, unexpectedly calm about the whole thing. Finally, McCain wore down.

"Just what do you expect of your career in the Navy, sailor?" he said.

"Not much, sir," said the sailor. "I muster out tomorrow."

McCain, who realized he had just wasted half an hour of his time, dismissed him in disgust. We loved it.

The *Pocono* was a 459-foot floating command post that carried advanced communications equipment and a complement of 490 men, including 54 officers. Overall we had a highly intelligent group of sailors. I was personnel and administrative officer, running the office for the captain and handling his mail, the orders we received, and all the enlisted men's and officers' records. I had regular office hours and then, as all officers did, stood watch, which meant a four-hour stint, from 8:00 to midnight, midnight to 4:00 a.m., or 4:00 to 8:00 a.m.

Every six weeks or so, we would spend two weeks at sea. We'd steam out of Norfolk on Monday, conduct readiness drills through the week, spend weekend leave at a port in Florida or the Caribbean, then steam back the following week, doing drills the whole time, and return to Norfolk on Friday.

My first time at sea was notable for the difficulty I had in getting my sea legs. I tried my best to walk across the deck without the enlisted men laughing at me, although I can't say I blamed them when they did. Then there was learning not to get seasick. The trick, I discovered, was not to stay below decks too long when we were under way. Work long enough at a desk where it's hot, stuffy, and disorienting, and you're going to get seasick. I did, and I had to go topside and vomit over the side. Yes, it was embarrassing. Then there were more basic matters, like lowering my spoon into a bowl and letting the rolling ship bring the soup to it, as the view through the porthole changed from sky to horizon to ocean and back again, over and over.

It soon became very clear why the course work I'd done was so rigorous. Beyond the basics of naval terms, there were times when I was the officer of the deck, temporarily in charge of the ship. I had to know things like the rules of the road for collision avoidance or what to do if there was a problem in the engine room—at least, I was supposed to know. My roommate, Dan Hecker, did, in fact, face a fire in the engine room while OOD. He called the entire ship to general quarters and got it handled. It was frightening to think about what might have happened had it been I. I could imagine the entire ship being awakened at night to hear me say, "Well, everybody, we have a fire in the engine room. What do you think we ought to do?" You can't "Aw, shucks" that one.

Once, I was Junior OOD when we got a request from the engine room to "blow tubes." I was fresh from Kentucky and I figured if your tubes need blowing, you should have at it, whether or not I knew what you were talking about.

"Permission granted," I said. Well, I had given them permission to clean the boiler tubes with a blast that would send black smoke and soot out into the open air. If the wind is blowing favorably, that's not a problem, but if it's blowing in the wrong direction, as it was that day, you have that mess lingering and settling on the forward deck, which, as it turns out, was just being painted.

My permanent quarters were shipboard even when we were in port, unlike some of the married officers, who got to go home at night. To get there, you walked down one flight of metal steps—everything was metal—past the wardroom, or mess cabin, and the lounge. You stepped over the raised bottom of the watertight door, called a knee knocker, into a passsageway leading to quarters. Mine was the first on the port side, which was to the right as you faced the back of the ship. It was maybe 15 feet by 20 feet, and I shared it with three other officers. You walked in and my rack was the lower forward one. Each of us had a countertop with a mirror on it and drawers underneath it. We each had a small closet and a built-in desk. There were three of those four-person quarters in our passageway. Across the passageway was the head and there were three more quarters across the passageway on the other side of that.

Learning leadership the Navy way was a long process. Part of it was negotiating the close quarters aboard ship. Officers and enlisted men had a forced proximity. My mother had always drummed into me the importance of being a friend to everyone, but that simply didn't work in a situation that called for some separation to maintain the respect necessary for discipline. Since it couldn't be a physical separation, it had to be one of bearing. You couldn't be a buddy and a leader. I needed a persona that elicited respect, and I needed to be cognizant of the kind of rapport I had with enlisted men.

Within that framework, the job you had often affected how you handled yourself. The boatswain's mates, for example, are the rowdy, rough-and-tumble men that do the grunt work topside, and the officer in charge of them really needs to be a man's man. If you're in administration, on the other hand, you have a more educated enlisted group and you can have a softer leadership style. I was more of a straight arrow than most of the other officers, keeping the line more rigidly drawn. It was just who I was.

I was company officer for the radiomen. They were skilled, prima donna types who were quite sophisticated at their gamesmanship, and I had to be respectful but forceful with them. It was an approach that was consistent with who I was, and there was no need for me to try to change to match someone else's approach. I'm not the shouting, screaming, cursing type, and so that wasn't the tack I took. I didn't use any of the foul language of the Navy, and I developed the reputation of being circumspect, as opposed to the guy who was in charge of the boatswain's mates, who cursed as they did.

There was one sailor aboard ship who was particularly hard to control. Everyone had trouble disciplining him. I brought him into my office after one infraction, had him sit down, and just looked at him. After about thirty seconds, I said to him, "Who in the hell do you think you are?" The guy broke down and cried like a baby. Now, any other officer would have started lambasting him, giving him a good cursing. But after a bit of silence, hearing me say the only four-letter word he'd ever heard me say just tore him up.

There was another sailor who was notorious for his unkempt appearance and for the fact that he never, ever showed up on time. I dealt with him by having him stand at attention once for thirty minutes before and after the admiral went ashore. Several high-ranking officers and six sideboys in sharp, respectful military lineup were paying their respects as the admiral departed ship, and then here was my sloppy sailor off to one side, standing at attention before, during, and after. He stood out like a sore thumb, and it was embarrassing enough for him that I didn't have any more trouble with him.

The one exception to my policy of rigid separation from enlisted men was one of our stewards, a large African American man. We'd go out for maneuvers on a Monday, drill all week, and then Friday we'd come in to shore, often at a very nice place. It could be a port in Florida, but it might be Bermuda, Nassau, or somewhere else in the Caribbean. Our steward would spend the entire weekend drinking, spending every dime he had, and he'd roll back to the ship around 4:00 a.m. on Monday and tell the cab driver to wait while he got the fare. He'd weave his way into the stateroom I shared with three other officers. I'd feel his towering if wobbly presence before I was fully awake, smelling the alcohol and sweat. He'd grab hold of me and shake me and I'd give him twenty bucks.

That was the one time I didn't insist on the proper respect due an officer, and in return I got far better service than anyone else in the wardroom. Any favor that could possibly accrue to an officer came my way first. No one quite understood why I got served before senior officers, and that was fine with me.

We traveled to plenty of interesting ports, and the admiral had his favorites. I remember one island with a part of town that was off-limits for American sailors. Each officer would get his men together and tell them, "You will not go 'over the hill' when you're ashore this weekend."

Several of the officers began talking about it during one visit, wondering what was over there. It actually sounded kind of neat, so a group of us headed that way. We walked into this big entertainment venue with a show that wasn't exactly family friendly. We sat down and there, three or four rows in front of us, were several of my men. They turned around and waved and I waved back and eventually one of them, normally a respectful, hardworking introvert, was drunk enough to go onstage and become part of the act. Of course, I couldn't say anything to them when we got back to the ship because I'd been there with them. I realized that they were really surprised that Mr. Turner had visited a place like that, but I think they were kind of proud of me too!

I had joined the Navy in part to be my own man, but it wasn't simple to escape my name. I learned that a sailor named Monty Lawrence was from Bowling Green, and I told him I was from Scottsville. He wrote home to his folks and said his company officer was a Mr. Turner from Scottsville, and they wrote back and said the only Turner they knew from Scottsville was Cal, who was loaded, or something to that effect. It wasn't long before I had numerous opportunities to loan money to sailors—opportunities that hadn't existed before that letter.

Our ship visited New York City at one point, and I thought this was a perfect opportunity to do something nice for Harry and Gladys Weiner, who always treated us royally when we visited New York and who by this time were practically family.

On this occasion, I invited the Weiners to have dinner in the wardroom of the ship, setting up a major clash of cultures. Harry had a big wide nose, wore horn-rimmed glasses, and smoked curli-cue cigars. It was cold when they came to visit, so Gladys, who was taller than Harry and wearing high heels, had on her full-length mink coat. They were quite the striking couple.

It happened that they came across the brow, the gangplank from the pier to the quarterdeck, as the admiral was about to depart, so there were sideboys everywhere, as well as full captains and other officers assembled to see him off. It was an impressive spectacle, and as Harry, who was trailing Gladys, got closer, he looked up and saw the officer on deck standing at attention and saluting. Harry, who never met a stranger but was unused to this kind of formal recogni-tion of his eminence, beamed, eyes lighting up under the hat sit-ting askew on his head, and said, "Hello dere," as the officer of the deck saluted. Despite the requirement for military decorum, it was all many of the sideboys could do to keep from cracking up.

But then we got to dinner in the wardroom, and Harry took full advantage of this opportunity to hold court. He informed us that as "a big taxpayer," he wanted to know what each of the officers did to justify his salary. I got more and more embarrassed as he questioned each officer about how much work he did and even, in some cases, how much he was paid! It says something about Harry that every-body liked him anyway.

As I finished those eighteen months in Norfolk, I wanted the adventure of an overseas assignment. I also knew I didn't want to end up in a tin can, which was what we called destroyers, since I didn't know much about ships and didn't want the kind of isolation or responsibility that went with becoming an executive officer. I called my mother's first cousin, Anna Belle Clement, who was chief of staff to Tennessee governor Frank Clement, her brother.

"I'd like to be assigned to Europe for the last year-and-a-half of my tour of duty," I said. "Is there anything you can do for me?" To this day I don't know whom she contacted, but she called me back and said, "Cal Jr., how does Thurso, Scotland, sound?"

"It sounds good to me," I said, although I'd never heard of it.

The United States Naval Radio Station outside Thurso was brand new. It was commissioned on January 3, 1964, six months before I got there. One of the northernmost bases in the world, it was part of a worldwide network called the Defense Communications System. We relayed signals to the North Atlantic, where communication with ships was really difficult to accomplish. The post was at the edge of a cliff on a rocky shore of the North Sea, with fewer than a hundred men in three buildings overlooking the Orkney Islands on Thurso Bay. There was always the sound of the wind and of the waves breaking on the rocks. There wasn't a tree anywhere—we always laughed that we were in the midst of "a lot of gregarious people and a lot of frustrated dogs." The temperature seemed to be the same year-round, but for some mysterious reason the horizontal rain of summer knew when to become the horizontal snow of winter. You had to learn to walk with difficulty into a strong, steady wind, or deal with a forceful push from behind.

The locals used the Orkney Islands to predict the weather: "If ye can see th' Orkneys, it's aboot to rain," they'd say. "If ye cannae see the Orkneys, it's r-rainin' a'r-ready." The other seasonal change was the amount of daylight, a pendulum that swung a lot further than it did in the continental United States. In the winter, the sun set by

3:30 p.m. In summer, it set just barely, and that wasn't until 10:30 p.m. or so. There would be a little bit of dusk and then the sun rose again. They had a midnight golf tournament every year, playing all night.

The landscape was bare and the soil rocky except for the big swatches of peat, which was like damp coarse carpeting. The only color to be found amid the drab government housing came from the front doors, which people painted all sorts of bright colors. Inside, it was a different story. That's where people's personalities really came out. They reveled in bold colors and patterns, and you'd see a lot of plaids and polka dots.

Life was a struggle; the fishermen faced a rough, cold, windy sea. That and the desolate environment made for tough people yet warm interpersonal relationships. The men and women were wonderful. They were outgoing and the culture was nurturing and supportive to both family and friends. You were never a stranger. If you showed up at someone's house close to dinnertime, you were supposed to sit down and eat with them. I remember my first Sunday afternoon there, driving down the coast with Harry Russell, one of the locals, stopping at the hotel in every little town. His wife, Netta, and the children, who were small, would go to the lobby, and Harry, my fellow officer and cottage mate John McGarrigle, and I would go to the bar and have drinks. I learned to sing the old Scottish songs and to drink Scotch neat. It was, if anything, even friendlier than Scottsville. The locals got a kick out of the "Yanks," which was what they called all of us. Of course, being from the South and being called a Yankee bothered me, but that's what they called us. It was my first exposure to a very different culture, a different society, and a different economy, and it was a delightful time in my life.

It took me quite a while to get used to the brogue, which was thicker than pudding. My mother and my brother, Steve, came to visit once—it was a high school graduation present for him—and

Mama called me at work one day. She was at my cottage and a work-man had come to refill the diesel fuel in the generator, the sole source of electricity. She couldn't understand a word he said and I had to help them get it done.

As much as I had to work to understand the locals, they had their own challenges with me. In fact, they kind of steered me into adjusting my pronunciations. I'd ask for hard-boiled eggs and they'd hear "balled" when I said "boiled." "It's boyled," they'd say. They adjusted enough pronunciations for me that when I got back to Kentucky, my family started calling me a Yankee—the Northern kind—because I'd lost a lot of the Southern redneck in my vocalizations.

The twists and turns of language made for one of the more interesting cocktail parties I've ever attended. I had gone with Netta and Harry Russell, two good friends from the north of Scotland. The husbands and wives were in two separate groups and I, being a bachelor, was standing with the wives. Netta and the others were talking about the rough day they'd had and I said, "I know exactly how you feel. I've had a rough day too. In fact, my fanny is dragging."

The ladies reacted with expressions that hovered between confusion and horror.

"Cal," said Netta, "what did you say?"

"I said, 'My fanny's dragging.'" All of them got red in the face and Netta said, in her thick brogue, "Cal, go ask Harr-ry what that wor-rd means."

I walked across the room.

"Harry," I said, "what does *fanny* mean?"

"Uch," he said. "It means *vagina*. Why do you ask?"

At that point, the innocent bachelor trying to carry on an empathetic conversation with the girls became someone who would henceforth warn friends headed to Scotland not to reference their fannies.

I did eat really well there. The local butcher shop had carcasses hanging on the wall and the meat was wonderful. You could get incredible fillets—there it's pronounced FILL-ets—and of course, there was plenty of lamb, since they raised them right there. I'd cook the lamb chops the way my grandma cooked fried chicken. I'd toss them in a paper sack with a lot of flour and seasonings to coat them, then drop them in hot grease in the skillet. It was great eating. We'd marinate the fillets in Italian dressing and put the oven on broil, cooking them up close to that red hot burner, making French fries to eat with them. We had good breads and wonderful fresh butter—the real stuff—and since it was damp and cold all the time, that bread and butter really hit the spot. In the restaurants we'd eat fresh salmon. Given all that great food, it's probably not surprising that I gained quite a bit of weight while I was there.

Now and then we had higher states of readiness, and during some of those I'd have charge of the whole command. That meant I was overseeing the men who monitored the communications gear serving ships steaming in the stormy North Atlantic. I'd have 36 hours on, with no sleep, then 12 off, three times in a row, and then have 48 hours off. Depending on the season, it would be pretty much light all the time or dark all the time, and days and nights got all jangled up.

Just as in Norfolk, I was the straightest arrow among the officers. Once I found the enlisted men playing cards when they were supposed to be monitoring all the communications equipment, so I had them get back to work. The chief petty officer came out in the passageway to tell me condescendingly, "Mr. Turner, Commander Godfrey and Lieutenant Buckley (the commanding officer and executive officer, respectively) allow them to play cards when they have the watch."

I said, "Well, Chief, I respect that, so when they have the duty, the men can play cards, but when I have the duty, there won't be any card playing. Do you understand that?"

"Yes, sir."

I don't know why I felt I was supposed to be so by the book. The career officers were more "what the heck" about it. I was just there for a while, but it was going to be done right when I was responsible.

I was personnel officer in Scotland, again just as I'd been in Norfolk. I took care of the paperwork, which included detailed records on every sailor, including fitness reports and officers' evaluations. There were occasional offbeat assignments, like my efforts to assist a Catholic sailor and his wife in getting their marriage annulled on the basis of his impotence. We were under a really tight deadline because the sailor had impregnated the daughter of the local sheriff, who was all over the command, demanding that this man marry his daughter. The sheriff wrote to our command asking for our official position on the matter. As personnel officer, I had to answer him and calm the waters without letting him know the man's current matrimonial state or anything else about him.

I poured all of my Southern concern onto the page, telling him how very aware we were of what a difficult time this was for his family and how we wanted to do everything in our power to help life go well for this couple. I got out the entire string section and conducted it very well, if I do say so myself. That letter came to the attention of the London-based admiral responsible for the U.S. Navy throughout Great Britain. He was so impressed that he called our commanding officer and told him to do everything he could to persuade Lieutenant (j.g.) Turner to consider a career in the Navy.

"He has great prospects for a successful Navy career," the admiral said. "I have never seen anyone able to say nothing so beautifully." It was an interesting take on what might foretell success in the Navy, but I took it as a compliment.

I wasn't tempted by a Navy career, and I came back across the Atlantic in December 1965, mustering out at the Brooklyn Naval

Shipyard after three years and four months. It was one of only a hand-ful of times my dad ever left his office in the warehouse in Kentucky, and he was waiting for me when the ship came in. He told everybody, "I will not be home until I bring Cal Jr.," and so he waited for the out-processing, which took three or four days, and the unloading of my stuff—a trunk, a player piano I'd bought from a hotel in the north of Scotland, and a Mercedes 220 I bought tax-free from a dealer in London. We got in that Mercedes and rode home together.

6

Interning with
The Real Cal Turner

My father had looked forward to the time I would come back and run the company, but neither he nor I knew what that would entail. Any father-son relationship is complicated, and conducting one while running a business makes it that much more so. Luther had died two years earlier, in 1963, and although my dad had run the show, essentially since the beginning, Luther was a huge presence in my father's life. His last years, as his dementia worsened, had been very difficult. I remember the last time my father really felt that he got through to him. Luther had lost most of his ability to communicate, but my father said, "Daddy, last year the company's earnings were one million dollars," and Luther chuckled.

Now, the son was the father. My dad was fifty, I was twenty-five, and this would be new territory. My dad's bottom line since the beginning could be summed up in one word—*survival*—and he reasoned that the key to survival in retailing lay in something his father had said. He'd quote him often—"If I control my expenses better than the competition, I just have to buy as well as he does—and I've got him!" That's why he watched the company's sales and expense reports so closely.

That approach kept the company going during its early years, but he realized it wasn't going to be enough in the future. My dad knew that for all the skills he brought to the company, there were others he didn't have. He was an entrepreneur, unschooled in business theory. He was aware of the gap between an entrepreneur and a seasoned leader and he wanted me to fill it. My dad had the practical savvy it took to run a business. I didn't. But he knew the company needed a different kind of leadership, and he believed that given my temperament, education, and experience, I was the likeliest one in the family to provide it. That meant we were going to have to deal with each other man to man as well as father to son, although it's difficult to take the father out of the father or the son out of the son.

My father and I had a great deal of love and respect for each other. He was a people-loving person, and he made no bones about his admiration for me. He was very proud of what I'd accomplished to that point, graduating cum laude (something else I couldn't pronounce until May 1962) from Vanderbilt University and serving three years and four months in the Navy, and he was eager to turn the family business over to his firstborn son. On the other hand, both of us were highly competitive and we were largely unaware of just how that might set us up for occasional conflict. In fact, we shared quite a few personality traits. Although his heart for others was as big as the outdoors, my dad was an intense man whose word was law. I was no shrinking violet myself, and I still had some of my Navy rough edges.

A bachelor at the time, I had moved into my parents' house for a while. The room and board were great, but the situation intensified our relationship. We were playing bridge one night with my mother and one of her friends, and my dad, in his own type A way, was being pretty aggressive, teasing and heckling me as we played. He may have been unaware that his competitive streak was so fully engaged. On the other hand, that may have been his message—"You're going to have to accept that I'm going to be overbearing." I took it for a while, but then I looked at him pointedly and, cleaning up the Navy language considerably, said, "Would you get off my butt?"

It was as if the earth had stopped. Very little could stun my father into silence, yet I had just done it. He was as shocked and upset as I had ever seen him; he looked as though he were going to cry, and seeing that, I wanted to cry. He folded his cards and set them down. We all did the same. It was obvious the game was over.

I'm not sure to this day why my words affected him so profoundly. I guess they seemed completely out of character for me, since this was probably the first pushback he had gotten from me as an adult, and he wasn't accustomed to any pushback at all. Yes, I had cleaned up the language, but in the Turner family home in Scottsville, Kentucky, those words from son to father were simply unacceptable. The very air seemed to turn frigid.

It wasn't any warmer the next morning. I knew I was going to have to do something. My plan was to approach him at work and render an apology with strings attached, the way most people do. I'd say I was sorry and tack on some qualifications, making it clear I expected him to apologize back.

My office was in one corner of the upstairs warehouse, above the ready-to-wear department. His was in the diagonally opposite corner. He had an executive washroom, and he was in it when I went into his office. I was relieved, because that meant I could apologize through a closed door. I stood outside and started talking, wrapping it up after a while with a soft, "...and so, Daddy, I'm sorry."

There was a long, long silence, worse than the one that had descended on the card table the night before. I stared at the door, from which nothing was forthcoming. Finally, he cleared his throat and said, "Son, I accept your apology." He let that sink in for a moment and then said, "You know, son, in any successful relationship, there has to be flexibility. However, in a father-son relationship, I don't think anyone should expect the *father* to be flexible!"

What in the dickens can I make of that? I thought. I walked back to my office.

I may not have understood it then, but that statement of my father's has stuck with me to this day. It's a truly important concept. Bringing me into J. L. Turner and Son meant major changes for the company, for my father, for me, and for our relationship. Inner flexibility is vital in dealing with change, and as a practical matter, I can never count on anyone else to have it, yet I should expect it of myself. My dad and I needed to find a way to move toward something closer to equal footing, but as much as he wanted that, it was hard for him. It was a process that continued throughout his life, and it was not always smooth sailing. I learned over and over the importance of being flexible, and of letting him be who he was. To this day, it feels as if he was wrong to have made such a big deal out of my comeback to him during that game of cards, but I was just going to have to accept that now and then he might pitch a fatherly fit. I had to learn not to push back because it was still, above all, a loving father-son relationship.

When I joined the company, my dad put me to work opening stores, figuring that one of the best ways to learn the business was to unload and stock everything we sold. I started full-time in December 1965 and helped open a store for the first time on my birthday in January. It was a small store in Camden, Tennessee, and I worked with three seasoned district managers, so it all went pretty smoothly. The next Sunday night I was sent to Anniston, Alabama, where I met Charles Richard Douglas, a new district manager. The store we were going to open was three times the size of the one in Camden, and there were only the two of us.

"Well, what do we do?" he said.

"What do you mean, 'What do we do?' This is only the second store I've opened!"

"Well, it's my first!" he said. I was flabbergasted and I called our head of operations, Walter Gupton. Walter had co-owned the junior department store in Munfordville, Kentucky, with J. L. Turner and Son, and he had sold it to them and come to work for the company. Walter had a full head of gray hair and wore black horn-rimmed glasses over blue eyes that sparkled when he laughed, which he did often. He was a genuinely nice person, although he was demanding.

"Walter," I said, "what do you mean sending me down here to open this big new store with Charles Richard, who hasn't even opened a store yet?"

He said, "Well, Cal Jr., the only thing I can tell you is that there are twenty-four hours in every day between now and Friday morning, when you need to have that store open at nine o'clock," and I realized that the boss's son was getting it stuck to him. We got it open, though, and as they did pretty much every time we opened a store for the next twenty years, people lined up at the door.

Eventually, over the course of the first couple of years, I was part of opening fifteen or twenty stores, and my dad was right. It was a good way to learn. We had four days to put one together from scratch, taking truckloads of merchandise as well as shelves and tables and moving them into a newly leased building. We'd start work first thing Monday morning, hiring people who came in off the street to help unload trailers, which were packed using the same method we used for managers' cars. My dad had the sides of the trailers lined with tables stuffed with merchandise that had been taken out of the boxes. We'd open the trailer and haul those heavily laden tables out and into the store.

The process started with Walter, who drew on graph paper the outline of each new store, then filled in the layout. He'd hand-draw the fixtures and pencil in the tables and shoe racks, the wall displays, the checkout and cash register, taking into account posts and the like. Then he'd add up all the tables and racks and figure how many linear feet of shelving we needed. The paperwork would go to the Chicken House (which is what it had been), a workshop where a team of carpenters manufactured and painted everything that went into those stores. The only thing we had to hire out in those days was the manufacture of metal racks for shoe displays. Installing all that stuff in a new store was never an exact science, though. Walter's layout would invariably miss an inset on this wall or a post in the middle of the floor, so we'd have to fit those tables in as well as we could. There would be leftovers and pieces that didn't fit, and they would get put back in the stockroom. In fact, at one point after I'd been there a while, we sent a trailer around to the stores to try to purge them of all that unused stuff, hoping the guys in the Chicken House could recycle it.

You had to be half carpenter to get everything installed, and then you had to take the merchandise, which would be spilling out onto the floor, and figure out how to get it all sorted, then displayed in time to have the store opened Friday morning. It was like creating order at the city dump.

We were famous—notorious, actually—for being able to do just that. When we opened our store in Cookeville, Tennessee, the local merchants were gathered in a drugstore, talking over coffee.

"You can't kid me," said one of them. "You don't receive two trailer loads of fixtures and two trailer loads of merchandise on Monday, two additional trailers on Tuesday, another on Wednesday, and have your store open on Friday."

"You've made one mistake," said another. "You don't know that damned Cal Turner bunch. They're crazy! There's no telling what they can pull off."

What made it all work was the trial-by-fire training that everyone—including me—received. The crew was always more than able to unload and stock the store by Friday, not to mention hiring local employees and training the manager.

The Cookeville opening did happen on Friday and it went so

well we needed a second checkout counter. Trouble was, we only had one cash register. Being the ingenious lot we were, we made a cash drawer out of a plastic cutlery tray we were selling in the housewares department. It had enough knife, fork, and spoon compartments for all the bills and coins and worked well enough. Of course, it gave that same group of businessmen more fodder for their gossip.

"That store won't last long," one said. "They can't even afford a cash register!"

Ingenuity took many forms. Once, Fel Myers, who had gone to school with my dad and had worked for him since the beginning, was opening a store in Pineville, Kentucky. He was having trouble getting electricity, and he called my dad and told him.

"Have you ever heard of Coleman lanterns?" my dad asked. Fel knew he'd better think of something, and he quickly found a solution that didn't involve lanterns.

Setting up that fast, we didn't have time to make sure everything met health codes, so those stores didn't have public bathrooms. They were for employees only.

We knew we had a winning formula and the vast majority of stores we opened did very well. Now and then, though, one would do poorly. We'd study it for a while, make whatever changes we thought necessary, and then give it another year or two to see if we could turn it around. We wrote three-year leases with three-year options, and that's about all it took to see whether a store was going to make it. After three years, if a store wasn't making money, we closed it, and while it took us four days to open a store, we could close one in a day and move on!

While I was opening stores, I got a letter in the mail from the U.S. Navy. It was a promotion! I had mustered out as a lieutenant junior grade, and the letter said I'd been made a lieutenant. I guess they figured I was more valuable to them out of the Navy than in it! I think if I'd have been anybody else, I'd have jumped at the chance to go back into the Navy as a lieutenant rather than open another Dollar General store, but there was that Jr. at the end of my name.

It wasn't long before my dad wanted me to go out with Walter and learn to negotiate leases for new stores. *Cheap* and *short-term* were the bywords. The rule of thumb was that we were not supposed to pay more than $1 a square foot per year, so that if there was a 5,000-square foot building available, we didn't want to pay any more than $5,000 a year.

"We don't have to have great locations," my dad said. "With our merchandise and our prices, we just need some kind of building around us. The concept conforms to the location. We will take almost any building and make it fit. We don't have stores built to our specifications because 'this is our model' or 'all our stores have to look a certain way.' So we feel we really are neighborhood stores because we conform to the neighborhoods in which we operate. It's the country general store cloned over and over."

Those two things—opening stores and negotiating leases—were the only bits of functional training my dad had thought of for me, since I already had years of warehouse and retail experience growing up. When I was back in Scottsville at our headquarters, I was supposed to do anything that needed to be done in the office or in the warehouse.

Actually, by that time, the company's real estate subsidiary, Goad Realty Company, Inc., owned three warehouses in Scottsville with a total of 155,000 square feet, and we leased a fourth, containing 60,000 square feet, from the Allen Realty Company, Inc., which had my dad as its sole stockholder. Each had its own loading dock, although often you'd see a truck being loaded through the front door, and drivers would have to make stops at several to get all the merchandise for delivery to a given store.

My dad wanted to hang on to the two things he loved the most— buying merchandise and watching weekly expenses by reading the reports prepared by the bookkeepers from the raw data coming in from stores and warehouses on expenses, inventory, and sales. I helped him monitor those reports, but when any personnel or administrative problem came up, or when there was anything that needed to be planned or organized, he wanted me to do that. I had the degree from Vanderbilt and my experience in the Navy. That gave me more training in those things he didn't want to do anyway.

Studying the numbers helped me hone my knowledge of how my dad looked at business. He strove to operate the stores at a gross margin of 16 ⅔ percent of sales. It was an outgrowth of the way he charged those $1 items to the stores. If an item sold for $1, he'd bill a dozen of them to the store at $10. The store would bring in $12, for a gross margin of $2, or 16 ⅔ percent. As long as their cost of business was below that, they were making money...Simple!

So my dad wanted to keep costs as a percentage of gross sales as follows: 3 percent for rent, 5 percent for payroll, 1½ percent for utilities, and no more than 1½ percent for shrinkage—loss of inventory from shoplifting, employee theft, administrative error, breakage, and the like. Those were the controllables, and every single percentage point of each of those had *better* be controlled. You controlled the rent when you negotiated that lease, and you simply couldn't build as cheaply as you could rent. As for the utilities, my dad was a firm believer in turning the lights off when you didn't need them. The one exception was the black and yellow electric *Dollar General* sign above every store. His desire to have store managers turn them off during the day was overruled by his fear that they wouldn't turn them back on again at night. Those signs were beacons to customers—even on cloudy days they looked great—and he didn't want to chance losing that extra bit of visibility, so he hard-wired them to stay on.

The rest of that 16 ⅔ percent of sales gave you a little room for advertising, supplies, and any other expenses, and anything left over was profit.

Those percentages were something my dad could keep a close eye on. Bookkeepers, working in Scottsville, handled twelve to fifteen stores each and gave him the reports he reviewed each week.

That 5 percent rule for payroll—if a store was bringing in $20,000 a week, it could spend $1,000 on payroll—placed us at the bottom of a low-paying industry. You needed two employees in the store at all times—at least, that's what we strove for. If business wasn't good and we had to control payroll even more rigorously, we'd have one person come in and open the store and stay there alone for a couple of hours before the second came in.

Each store had a manager and clerks. We tried to establish pay scales system-wide, and you had to pay minimum wage, but market conditions had an effect and there was some local variation. Below a certain wage, you couldn't attract hardworking people. So a manager had to work hard to find that balance. And the manager kept 10 percent of the store profit as a bonus, which meant that getting sales up and bringing payroll in at, say, 4½ percent of annual revenue, meant more money in his or her pocket.

The code of ethics for store managers and everyone above them was pretty straightforward: *Work hard. Be honest. Don't drink on the job. Don't screw the help.* Just two months after I came to work for J. L. Turner and Son, those rules helped me out of my first painful company decision. One of our district managers had shown up in a store drunk. It just so happened that visiting the store was a saintly couple who traveled to our stores taking inventory. They quickly placed a call to my dad, who was out of town, which meant the call came to me. I was going to have to fire this man. What a wretchedly awful thing to experience for the first time!

I wasn't very good at it. I went through a lot of apologetic explanation, which is not the way you handle firing somebody. You just make the announcement and let the person adjust to it. In this case, I did the adjusting. I was aware of how hard this was on him, but I was self-conscious enough that I was much more aware of how hard it was on me!

My dad hated letting people go, so through the years I was the go-to guy when it came to firings. I never did like it much more than I did that first time, but I did get better at getting through it.

I learned a great deal in those days, but I still spent a lot of time scratching my head over how the company really worked. I quickly realized that meant learning how my father worked, and it wasn't going to be easy. My dad was an accomplished entrepreneur who couldn't quite explain how he made decisions. He just had to give you specifics in an ad hoc way. He had been living and breathing J. L. Turner and Son for a quarter of a century, and it seemed to be more in his gut than in his head. He had a lifetime of trial-and-error experience, and a lifetime of paying attention to the way others did business, that went into every decision. Now, for the first time, he had another person at his side trying to learn what he knew, and it was almost as if we were speaking two different languages. I was looking for the cognitive, for an analyzable version of something that came naturally and that he'd never had to explain to anyone before. He was more attached to the doing than the discussing. My dad was a reservoir of great insights whose primary outlet was the work. I would have to learn by watching.

7

Dealing with Entrepreneurial Chaos

When my dad brought me into the company, he was eager to hand over the reins. At the same time, he had in the back of his mind that he was always going to be the strong background advisor to Cal Jr.— as his father had been to him.

In fact, my dad never understood the distinction between family and business; they were one and the same to him. That made for a very interesting dynamic. We had the same name and a great deal of love and respect for each other, but I was still his son and it is the nature of father-son relationships that conflict is inevitable.

There were now two strong personalities under one business roof. My dad was not interpersonally aggressive, but he was so intense in his dedication to work that the people around him had all they could do just to keep up. Once, as we drove from the house to the warehouse, I was sharing with him that I was having a hard time getting along with a certain employee. He said, "I can understand that."

"How can you understand that?" I said.

"Son," he said, "how many employees do we have?"

"Around twelve hundred," I said.

"Do you realize that among all twelve hundred employees, there is just one I have trouble getting along with?"

"Well, Daddy," I said, "do you realize that of all twelve hundred employees, there is only one who will tell you the truth?"

A knowing grunt was all I got from him.

My dad had the innate assumption that if somebody didn't agree with him, that person just wasn't listening. He assumed he knew what was right. I would say to him, "Anytime we disagree, you can rest assured I listen even harder to you than when we agree, and I'm really careful when I proceed in a way you don't want us to proceed."

I was not interested in conflict for its own sake. I was there to learn. If I had come in to J. L. Turner and Son hungry for power, I never would have gotten to first base with my dad or the company. As a matter of fact, he was more interested in transferring power than I was in accepting it, because I recognized that I didn't know enough about the business. My dad was saying, in essence, "You just take this. Go with it." What I saw was a steep learning curve, with my being a Cal Sr. intern.

I knew, though, that nobody else in the company was privy to that mind-set. What they saw started and stopped with the fact that I was the boss's son. My mother had made me conscious of other people and how I came across to them, and I knew that in this case, human nature would make for a great deal of resentment. What they didn't know was that I was as put off by the role of boss's son as they were. I knew that nobody wants to follow the guy brought into the role by birth, and that I would never be able to prove myself. I was under scrutiny all the time, probably even more so than I'd been in the Navy, where the enlisted men were always testing me. And here again it was about passing the test. People would be analyzing how I said things and how I handled situations.

I spent a good deal of time observing my dad's leadership style. On store visits, he could seem stormy or cantankerous in his intensity to get things done the way he wanted, and he had a knack for going directly to the thing that was wrong in a store. I didn't want that to be my style. I didn't know enough about retailing to know in detail how they were supposed to do store work anyway. He did.

There was no detail too small for his attention, and he didn't point out a problem without having a solution. If he found a smudge on a piece of soft goods, he would get out his handkerchief. He knew that trying to rub it off with your hand or a brush would make it worse, but if you whacked it just right with a cloth, you could get out most of the smudge.

He wanted quick results. He was fast and efficient and he wanted others to be that way. He could be impatient; he didn't intend to be hard on people, but he was so single-mindedly focused on getting work done that he came across as harsher than he was. He didn't realize it, but Mama, for one, did.

"Cal, I'm not going to visit another store with you if you're going to be that mean," she once told him.

"I was not mean," he said.

"Cal, we've left the store, but the manager is in the stockroom crying right now."

My dad would just be amazed in moments like that. He simply couldn't understand that that was how he had come across.

He never slowed down. He didn't trust other people who did either. I know for a fact that he wasn't manic-depressive because he was never anything other than manic. Just as they had when I was a child, people were still saying that he was always on the brink of burning himself out or having a heart attack.

My dad's longtime banker, Sam Flemming at Third National in Nashville, was one of the few who talked about it to his face. It happened once when my dad went to Sam for yet another loan.

Sam said, "Now, Cal, I'm not making this loan to J. L. Turner and Son. I'm making a loan to Cal Turner, and I'm concerned about your health. You're overworking. The next time you come in here for a loan, I'm going to ask you whether or not you've cut back, and I'm going to want an answer."

The next time my dad came in, Sam said, "All right, Cal. I told you I was going to ask you this. Have you cut back on your workload?"

"Yes, Sam, I have," he said. "Laura and I have talked it over and our decision is for me to stop working on Saturday nights."

He'd been making those Saturday night calls to stores for years. He did indeed give them up, but it wasn't as if he did it for Sam or for his health. By the early to mid-sixties, the company was big enough that it was too much for him to keep up with every store. He would read every report, but he wouldn't make the calls anymore. He had also gotten to the point where he decided it was best not to be so stretched on cash that he had to sweat it down to the penny.

Still, Sam was satisfied with his answer, and like so many people who worked with Cal Sr., he had another good story to tell!

Meanwhile, I knew I had to get a handle on the workings of the business, but more and more I realized it was just as important for me to get a handle on my own approach to leadership.

Every potential leader has strengths and weaknesses, and I had to come to grips with mine. We all have barriers to get past, and mine was right there at the end of my name. As much as I wanted to be my own man, I understood what it meant to be Cal Turner, Jr. It wasn't just the potential for resentment. It was also the potential for undue expectation. I was in some sense the prince being trained by the king. Success would not likely be attributed to me because everything had been handed to me. Failure, on the other hand, would largely be mine alone.

People can resent the prince in those circumstances, but they also expect him to have the answers and the power. They would expect Cal Jr. to be fully grounded in authority when in reality, of course, I was not. I certainly did not sense that much ground underneath myself!

As much as that scenario seemed to put me in a lose-lose situation, though, it turned out to be a rare advantage, prodding me toward a career-positioning philosophy that helped me in major ways throughout my business life.

Leadership exists when an organization overcomes having a boss or a boss mentality. A boss only gets results; a leader gets development. And it is necessary for a leader to get over him- or herself. I had to get over being the boss's son, and it seemed to me that the best way to do so was to poke fun at myself *as* the boss's son. It was a throwback to my mother's efforts to get me to take myself less seriously, and it became part of my management style. I'd say, "I'm over my head here and I need your help. I have such great respect for what goes on in a store because I've tried most of the jobs in the company and I'm not good at any of them."

It was an approach that grew out of the genuine respect I had acquired for the people who do those jobs. They understand the business better than any of us because they understand the customer better. I knew we ought to bring their insight into what we were doing with the company—that, I realized, was a key to effective leadership.

This thing called authority works only when it's shared with everybody. A true leader vests the authority in the organization. My objective was to convince people that I really wanted them to tell us the truth, and I knew the greatest truth was what we got from our customers by way of our employees. In a retail company, the real authority lies with the customers, and you respond to them collectively. The leader responds to the employees, who respond to the customer. Trying to get out from under my role as boss's son positioned me to do that much better than I might have otherwise.

Which was a very good thing, because as I looked at the company I'd just been appointed to lead, I knew I was walking into entrepreneurial chaos. The company had essentially no

organization—everything was within the gut of the founding entrepreneur. If the company had drawn up an organizational chart in
those days, it would have been a circle, with my father at the center
and lines radiating out in all directions. We had no board. We didn't
have a CFO. We had no annual budget or consolidated financial
statements. Once a week we got an operating report on every store
and on our warehouses, and the auditors came in twice a year from
the Louisville office of Lybrand, Ross Bros. & Montgomery, which
eventually became PricewaterhouseCoopers, and put together our
quarterly financial reports, something they could never do today,
since there's a strict line between preparing the statements and
auditing them.

There was another interesting aspect to our financial reports,
and it was something I discovered as I talked to my dad about shrinkage, merchandise or cash that has been stolen, lost, or otherwise
unaccounted for. I was adamant that we had to control it and we
couldn't because of the way he handled the books. Sometimes when
we bought an item for, say, $6 a dozen, he'd make an entry that said
we paid $8 for them. That created an overage that would offset some
of the inevitable shrinkage, giving him a cushion he could bring to
bear on the year-end numbers. If he overdid it, though, our auditors
would come to him about our warehouse overage for the year. He'd
say, "Well, we don't need to show that much profit," and he'd start
subtracting from the overage and save it for the next year.

Was that legal? We didn't know and didn't think about it. I knew
it was inaccurate accounting, and my beef with him was that that
overrode our shrinkage, so we could never really get a handle on
it—for management, it was out of sight and out of mind. "Daddy,
we've got to control shrinkage," I said, "and we can't control it if we
don't know what it is. The way you're handling the books, you're cov-
ering it."

"Son," he said, "in retailing, you're never going to be able to control your shrinkage completely, no matter what you do. You're always going to have a surprise at the end of the year, and I'm going to see to it you have a positive surprise."

He was convinced it was the right way to do it, and I had to accept it.

It was one of many aspects of the business I viewed as chaotic and my dad or others viewed as business as usual. It amazed me how much chaos there was in what had by then grown to a 150-store chain. You have to have a sense of something else, an outside norm, in order to recognize chaos *as* chaos, and I guess that's part of what I brought to the equation.

Now, chaos can be threatening or empowering. In my case, I'd have to say it was empowering in the sense that it made me realize how badly I needed management training, especially in light of the fact that, in 1968, when I'd been with the company for three years, my dad decided it was time to take it public. The target date was December of that year, and in the fall I signed up for the American Management Association's management course in New York. The AMA studied and taught management; it had a whole catalog of courses in various fields, from accounting for the nonfinancial executive to sensitivity training.

I first heard about the AMA through Don Marsh of Marsh Supermarkets in Indiana. Marsh, also a family business, was upgrading its stores, moving to bigger buildings in a number of towns, and the company wanted to talk to a noncompetitor like us about leasing those buildings. I visited Don, who was just a little older than I, and then he came to Scottsville, visiting our headquarters and having dinner with us while I was still living on Cherry Street with my parents. He talked about how useful the AMA had been and he mentioned the "Management Course" in particular. I was trying to determine the management and development needs of the company and thought this sounded like something I needed. I knew that a better understanding of management as a profession, and grounding in leadership principles, would be good for me.

The course consisted of four weeks—one month of good, solid management fundamentals—and it showed me how little I knew about management. I was particularly impressed with Larry Appley, the AMA's charismatic chairman and guru. He addressed a large auditorium full of management trainees and wowed us with his views on management as a profession, in a league with law and medicine. Like them, it had a code of ethics and well-established principles and disciplines.

As he elaborated on its challenges and its importance, his words resonated very deeply with me. I thought my mandate was to help J. L. Turner and Son evolve into a company with professional management, and Appley's characterization both excited and challenged me. My dad understood that we needed professional management to grow and develop long-term, and he relied on me to figure out how to do it.

My dad's decision to go public had come with pretty much no warning. He just said, in June of that year, "I'm ready." Selling stock would allow him to raise capital he needed for expansion. He also had his eye on the higher net worth that comes with company stock being valued at a multiple of its earnings rather than just its book value, the net assets of the company as reflected on its books.

We were on a great run. Sales had nearly doubled from $16 million in 1963 to $31 million as we approached this stock offering. This would allow our family to diversify, since we could sell some stock and invest elsewhere so we wouldn't have all our eggs in one basket.

We would be selling 27 percent of the company, with the family holding on to 73 percent. As we did so, my dad decided we should change the name, in keeping with the names of the stores we'd been launching since 1955. We would no longer be J. L. Turner and Son. We would be Dollar General Corporation. I accepted the change with regret, because I hated for the Turner name to come down. It took a while, but later I realized it was a good decision.

It was time to choose a board of directors, the governing body of a company tasked with looking over management's shoulders on behalf of the shareholders—ideally, at least. Actually, we chose directors, but just as a formality. We tried to look as good as possible on paper, but we never had a board meeting, and it was only later that we took that part of the business seriously.

We had six months to prepare for the sale. Jerry Kohlberg of Bear Stearns, who had handled the proposed public offering in 1962, handled this one as well. When that earlier one had been aborted, Jerry had proposed and arranged a loan from a syndicate of insurance companies, with the Turner and Son attorney, Don Oresman of Simpson Thacher & Bartlett, drawing up the papers.

Those loan agreements contained certain covenants that really helped the company mature between 1962 and 1968. For instance, my dad had to pay off the bank loans for one month a year, forcing him to plan a little better and run a tighter ship. The company was constantly underfinanced because of his tendency to overbuy. He acknowledged only one limiting factor when it came to buying.

"My inventory control," he used to say, "is the four walls of the warehouse," meaning he couldn't buy any more than we could stuff into our actual storage space. My grandfather was always concerned about overexpansion, but my dad knew he had to keep opening new stores because he was always buying more than the stores needed, taking all the seller had in order to get the lowest possible price. Of course, once he had more stores, he'd overbuy for *them*, too, which meant he had an even bigger need for cash, since buying really soaked it up. So, even though sales and profits kept growing, that ever-increasing inventory investment kept driving him back to the bank. The fact that he could borrow so much so often led him to laugh about how retailers could pull the wool over a banker's eyes. A retailer would ask to borrow money to open a second store in order to sell there what might not sell in just one store. Bankers, he said, didn't understand that if it isn't selling in store number one, it isn't going to sell in store number two!

Fortunately, my dad was as lucky as he was good. His habit of overbuying was supported by the expanding economy—he could simply expand with it. Most companies today don't have the success prospects that J. L. Turner and Son and then Dollar General Corporation had in those decades after World War II.

My grandfather had long been the conservative influence on my father. "Son," he would remind my dad constantly, "you cannot pay the banks six percent interest all of the twelve months a year and stay in business!" When he died in 1963, the insurance companies took over his role, doing their best to put at least that one-month brake on my father every year.

As we prepared for the sale, my dad, who generally avoided doctors, had to get an insurance physical. He went to see Dr. Ben Alper, a terrific internist in his early forties. Dr. Alper was so impressed with my dad that he bought stock in the company. He held on to it and was always very happy with its appreciation in value. (Of course, confidence in management is always a good reason for investing!)

We were all a little nervous about this offering, wanting it to go well. Don Oresman came to Scottsville and spent a lot of time working on the documents. My mother's brother, Frank Goad, who was an attorney in Scottsville, was instrumental in helping to get us ready, and Hubert Craddock, our secretary-treasurer, capped his contributions with an all-nighter before the morning we actually went public. I even got a secretary to help out. I'd used Earline Frost, one of the bookkeepers, when I needed someone to take dictation, standing beside her amid all those bookkeepers with their noisy calculators as she took down what I said. During the run-up to the public offering, we pulled her off bookkeeping and she came to work full-time for me.

Finally, when Bear Stearns was ready, Don went to the Securities & Exchange Commission in Washington and presented the documents so they could okay the sale of Dollar General stock to the public. Once they approved, he'd call Bear Stearns and DG would be a public company. The last document to be turned over to the SEC was a certified check for the registration fee. Don handed them the check, issued by the Farmers National Bank in Scottsville.

The clerk looked at it, looked at Don, and looked at the check again.

"We can't accept this," she said.

"Why not?" he said. "The regulations say you need a certified check, and that's a certified check."

"This isn't stamped *certified*," she said. "It's stamped *good*."

Now, the reason for that was Marguerite McClellan, a tiny, well-loved, big-eyed, and occasionally outspoken bundle of energy who ran her loan desk at Farmers National with an iron will. She was a vice president and she had determined at one point that she did not like the word *certified*. "What the hell does that mean?" she said. "We use the word *good*, as in *This. Check. Is. Good.*, and we have an officer sign or initial it. So what if the rest of the world doesn't do it that way? We're right, they're wrong!"

Well, I don't need to tell you that the SEC didn't see it that way. The entire process stopped, and we spent a couple of very nervous hours as Don went to his firm's Washington office and had them scurry to prepare a certified check that actually said *certified*.

Not long after that happened, I went to Marguerite and said, "You have to change the way you do certified checks! It held up our stock sale!"

She said, "Cal Jr., you and your family may own control of the Farmers Bank, but that doesn't mean you have control of Marguerite McClellan. This check is *good* and we're not going to change it."

And they didn't, until after Marguerite retired.

The stock sold at $16.50, and the company and Cal Sr. raised about $1.5 million, which we used to buy inventory and open more stores. The sale had a major effect on both my dad and me—on him because he sold some of the stock he owned, and on me because I was in the perhaps unenviable role of being responsible for a public company that had no chief financial officer, no budget, no planning, and scarcely any consolidated financials. Still, I wasn't as nervous as I should have been. I had the overconfidence of youth. My dad had the overconfidence of the entrepreneur, and he probably had overconfidence in his son. We really didn't know what we were getting into!

For starters, a lot of previously undisclosed information was now public. Quite a few of the people who had watched us grow now owned stock, and every six months they were going to get a report on sales and earnings, numbers that had been available only to the family and the bankers who lent us money. I soon realized it would be up to me to let them know how we were doing. I also had the responsibility of communicating with the analysts who would follow the company.

In January, a month after we'd gone public, somebody mentioned that we needed to do an annual report on the year that had just ended.

"What's an annual report?" I said. We were a public company and I honestly didn't know. Somehow I'd gotten through four years of Vanderbilt and earned a degree in business administration and didn't remember hearing the term. I had studied accounting, but our case studies were about the operations of companies, not annual or quarterly reports. There was a course on stocks and markets, but I never did take it. Now, however, there was an annual report due, and it was my baby. We took inventory of the stores and warehouses, and Lybrand, Ross Bros. & Montgomery audited our financials. I went into my office, closed the door, and wrote the narrative. Fortunately, the news was good, and it took me just six short paragraphs to spell it out in terms of profitable growth, which really described our company. Our net sales had increased 28 percent, to $40.5 million, and our net income had risen 37 percent to nearly $1.4 million. Both sales and income had doubled since 1964. I welcomed our new shareholders, gave them those figures, credited "the influence of our past," and told them two things I thought were very impressive:

1. A typical new store opened in less than a week and turned a profit in less than two months.
2. A typical existing store showed a gain over the previous year in both sales and profit.

It took just eight pages to give them all the charts, graphs, and history we needed to fill out the picture. There may have been times when it didn't seem as if we knew exactly what we were doing, but as the report pointed out, we were doing very well.

Sometimes life throws a lot at you at once, and as I dealt with going public and my first management training under fire, I was also preparing to get married. Margaret was almost six years younger than I, and no one who has ever seen her wonders why I was attracted to her. She is a sensitive and intelligent, poetically articulate person, and she has a natural class about her. I had first spotted her as she settled into a pew as part of the Park City, Kentucky, delegation to a sub-district meeting of the Methodist Youth Fellowship, although she was too young to pay attention to. I was president of our sub-district group, comprised of the churches from a number of little towns in the area. I think she would say she was impressed with me, too, and was drawn to the confidence I exuded, even if she thought I may have overexuded now and then. (Imagine that!)

After I'd gone through college and the Navy and had come into the business, I took my mother and my aunt Ruth to a concert at Van Meter Hall on the campus of Western Kentucky University in Bowling Green. Margaret and her mother came to the concert and just happened to sit in the row right in front of us. Her mother knew mine growing up, and Margaret and I got reacquainted. I eventually called her and asked her on a date. I remember that when Wayne Dugas, my brother-in-law, met her, he said, "Cal Jr., you'll never get this one. She's too good looking." I also remember how good it felt, on those first dates, when I got to put my arms around her. Somehow, we just fit.

Two years later, I asked her to marry me not long after a triple date we had with my sister Betty and her husband, Don, and my brother, Steve, and his wife, Judy. The five of us had left Scottsville to pick up Margaret in Bowling Green so we could all have dinner there. The drive over was a great one, and when Margaret got in the car, Steve said, "Margaret, we've had so much fun on the way over here, it's a shame you don't live in Scottsville too."

"Well," she said, "nobody's asked me." The others let out a great roar, and it wasn't long before we were engaged. Our marriage, on March 1, 1969, was a great relief to my mother, who had an interesting take on my bachelor days. When I was twenty-seven and still single, she had said, "Son, I'm afraid you're not going to get married in time."

"What do you mean?" I said.

"Let me explain life to you," she said. "A boy is under his mother's control until he gets to a certain age. After that, his mother can't control him. In fact, he's out of control from that time until he gets married, and then his wife assumes the job of control. I'm worried that you will have too much of a span of time between them and will be too far out of control when you finally get married; your wife will not be able to get you back into control."

"Mama, I didn't know that the function of marriage was control of the husband."

"Well," she said, "now you know!"

I look at my marriage to Margaret as taking place at just the right time, and more than one person has told me that when we're together, they can tell that after nearly fifty years we're still sweethearts, and they are right about that.

8

❧

Winging It with Wall Street

Writing that first annual report convinced me I didn't want to handle the company's public relations myself. In fact, there was a great deal about PR and marketing I didn't understand; the one marketing course I had in college hadn't made much of an impression on me.

In my early days with the company, I didn't need to know much to get press attention; our success drew plenty of that. One of the many reporters who came to interview me was the Louisville *Courier-Journal*'s business editor, Rod Wenz. He and I hit it off really well, and I felt comfortable confiding in him.

"Rod," I said, "we're a public company and we don't know what we're doing when it comes to PR. Do you have any suggestions?"

Rod thought about it and called a couple of days later.

"I've got a good idea," he said. "Why don't I freelance and do your PR for you?" He had done PR work for Chrysler during a stint as a reporter in Illinois, and I said I thought it was a great idea. Working from home, he wrote our press releases and then our quarterly and annual reports. If I had to make a presentation to analysts, he'd help me write the speech and prepare the slides. He eventually left the paper and, with Randy Neely, set up the Wenz-Neely Company, which went on to become Kentucky's largest PR firm, with clients including Kentucky Fried Chicken and the Louisville International

Airport. I always liked the fact that Dollar General was a client of Rod Wenz before he even formed a company.

I often wished I could have found a Rod Wenz to help in dealing with Wall Street. At one point in 1969, one of our big investors, Bankers Trust, wanted to talk, so I went to New York, where I sat down with three of their executives. They kicked off the discussion by saying, "We own a hundred thousand shares of your stock, and after this meeting with you, we will decide whether to sell the hundred thousand we own or buy another hundred thousand." I suddenly realized I was playing very high-stakes poker. Theirs was probably the most sizable block of stock outside our family at the time. I had to convince them that they'd been wise to invest in the first place and that the best thing they could do was to increase their stake.

They started asking questions, assuming, of course, that I could answer them. The truth was that I couldn't. All the financial information I had was in the form of those weekly reports on our stores and warehouses. "Would you like to know how we're doing in Arab, Alabama?" I could have asked them. "I've got the figures right here."

Normally, you would pull all those figures together, but we didn't yet have consolidated statements, and there was no financial analysis. There wasn't a CPA in the company.

So when they asked about, say, return on invested capital, I didn't have an answer, but I didn't want them to know that! I decided that taking a stab in the dark was better than giving no answer at all, so that's what I did. I took wild guesses about what the correct numbers might be. Then, when I got back to Scottsville, I went through the process of figuring out the real answer. Subtracting my guess from the true number gave us our performance gap, which in turn gave us our marching orders. It was no way to run a public company, but that's the way we did it then. From the time I joined the company in 1965 until I was named president in 1977, I winged it with Wall Street.

And by the way, I was so engrossed in running the company, I never did check to see if Bankers Trust bought more! That was the pace I was keeping then. I didn't have time for reconnaissance; I was already on to the next battle. And the only time we really thought about our stockholders was when we settled up twice a year (later, four times a year) and issued our reports.

We were a solid company. Our numbers were really good. My dad was on top of the business, store by store, week by week, so Dollar General was a successful retail venue. Still, New York didn't understand us. They viewed us as a company outside the normal parameters of retailing. Dollar General wasn't a dime store like Woolworth or a department store like J. C. Penney, so they couldn't categorize us. We weren't a conventional retailer at all. We bought opportunistically and sold what we found at even-dollar prices. Normally, an analyst would compare our price-earnings ratio to that of others in our sector, but we weren't really part of a sector.

One of the questions posed was about merchandise continuity. They knew that my dad had a way of finding one-of-a-kind deals and that a good percentage of our merchandise was closeouts and irregulars. "What happens," an analyst would ask, "as manufacturers get more efficient and there aren't any more irregulars or when the deals dry up? You're bottom-feeders, and so what happens when nothing is dropping to the bottom?" I pointed to our record of success in finding deals year after year and in having our customers accept them. "Our numbers speak for themselves!" I'd tell them.

"How are we going to be sure that's going to continue?" they'd say. At that point I'd do my best to change the subject. We kept bobbing along that way, and they always wound up being sold on us after the fact. Eventually, I guess the numbers *did* speak for themselves.

In the meantime, we had to come up with ways to keep them engaged. For instance, we'd schedule lunches in various cities, inviting analysts and investors so we could tell them about the company—and, we hoped, convince them to invest or recommend us. The trouble was it was hard to get them to show up. These were high-stakes meetings, so I decided to sweeten the deal, trying to make points by working with what I had. The next invitation that went out said, "If you'll let me know your size, I'll bring you a golf shirt—one of our irregulars, which I don't think you'll be able to tell from first-quality merchandise you'd buy in a high-end department store."

They usually couldn't tell the difference, and it worked well enough to attract a full house and the attention of *The Wall Street Journal*, which thought it was a clever approach and did a small front-page piece.

Still, I remember grumbling to my secretary, Earline Frost, about the fact that it was selfishness rather than the desire to understand the company that brought them to the meetings.

"Well," she said, "let me ask you this. If you had several luncheon invitations and one offered you a golf shirt and the others didn't, which would you accept?"

"Okay, I get it," I said.

Much of what we did was that way. My dad couldn't sift out what he knew and teach it, and I didn't know Wall Street. An entrepreneur can be one of the most creatively adaptive persons you'll ever meet, but it may not be cerebral. He is probably acting and reacting without too much thought to pattern or structure. He has a philosophy and experience but often not much else. It would take the concept of strategic planning to give us a road map for turning that from-the-hip genius into a solid approach to doing business, and that was still a long way off.

In the meantime, we had entrepreneurial, seat-of-the-pants growth. That was Daddy's style, and if New York didn't understand it, small towns all over the South did. They were the backdrop, the grounding reality, of the company, and the people in those towns loved the stores.

No town grounded us more than Scottsville, whose people never put on airs about our success. Analysts would come to town and ask directions to the headquarters of Dollar General.

"I don't know," someone would tell them, "but the Turner place is down East Main Street, next to Bob Graham's furniture barn."

Then there was the time the townspeople of Scottsville bailed us out. One Saturday at noon, lightning struck the tobacco barn warehouse and the sprinkler system ruptured. Water went all over the place, and since the merchandise was on the floor rather than on pallets, we knew practically all the soft goods would get wet. Word spread through the town that we had a problem and people came and volunteered to help. We worked until 10:00 p.m. Saturday getting merchandise out of the water and hanging it up—I can still see the long johns hanging on makeshift clotheslines outside. Then most of those people came back Sunday morning and did it again. Practically the whole town was out to help us recover. The pride they had in our success was best expressed by that kind of teamwork, and that continues to be a very moving memory to this day!

My dad had a great measure of resourcefulness when it came to salvaging merchandise. Part of it was just unwillingness, no doubt a result of his family's poverty-stricken days on the farm, to see anything go to waste. He once bought a truckload of wet socks from a fire sale in Nashville, and for two days, employees sorted and hung them all over the warehouse. When bell-bottoms went out of style, he had them cut off so we could sell them as shorts. He was always buying blouses and tops at the end of the season, just about the time other stores were no longer selling them.

His love of great buys was still a foundational element. Some of them took on mythic proportions. Once, before I came to the company full-time, he bought 35,000 fruitcakes at the end of the Christmas season. He just couldn't resist the price. I think the population of Scottsville was 2,500 at the time, and when the truck driver hauling those fruitcakes pulled into town, he stopped and called the dispatcher.

"Man, you have really screwed up," he said. "I have got a load of thirty-five thousand fruitcakes and this town doesn't have three thousand people. You must have sent me to the wrong place." We sold all of them, by the way, for a dollar each the next Christmas.

Then there was the time I walked into my dad's office and he had big piles of this synthetic fabric all over his desk. There was pink and blue and yellow, and it couldn't be folded, so it lay there in globs, looking like brightly colored amoebas. Obviously someone had gotten stuck with a lot of it and had given him a deal.

"What do you think of this, son?" he said.

"What is it?" I said.

"I don't know but I just bought it."

"Are you kidding me?"

He said, "Son, I bought this for a penny a yard. I'll buy *anything* for a penny a yard."

"What'll our customers do with that, Daddy?"

"I don't know, but we have smart customers, and they'll figure out something to do with it at that price."

Actually, they never did figure it out. That fabric wouldn't pile up—you'd put it on a counter and it would slide off onto the floor. Those bright pastel colors showed dirt easily, and so we wound up throwing much of it away. It was one of the few times my dad's intuition really missed.

Once, he bought hundreds of thousands of slippers at a dime a pair. Another time he bought all the clear plastic sandals a manufacturer had for 35 cents a pair. Then the fellow found out he had another warehouse or two of them. My dad didn't want his competition getting hold of them, so he bought those, too, for 25 cents a pair. Then, whether by design or not, the fellow found he had some more—in a warehouse in Jamaica—and my dad bought those for 11 cents a pair. We had them coming out our ears!

"But it was a good buy," Daddy would say in situations like that. "If I have to declare bankruptcy, I won't be embarrassed to tell the judge what I paid for this inventory I can't get rid of."

He missed on hula hoops too. He bought them by the carload just as the fad ended and finally traded them to another company.

At bottom, though, the company wouldn't have done as well as it had if there hadn't been a real method to his madness. One of the best examples involved his decision to stock irregulars. When we got in the dollar store business, my dad knew that our customers appreciated a well-made garment and he knew the huge quality difference between the clothing of the good manufacturers and that of the low-end manufacturers, who would cut corners to achieve low prices. So he reasoned that the irregulars of a good manufacturer were worth more than the first-quality product of a schlock manufacturer, and that our customers would appreciate that. An irregular garment might not meet the high standards of big merchandisers like Sears or J. C. Penney, but their imperfections were normally so slight they couldn't easily be detected—which was why handing them out to investors and analysts was so effective. So my dad negotiated contracts with manufacturers, saying, "I'll take every irregular you have at this percentage of your price." He knew the good manufacturers were on top of style, fabric, color, and quality, so he didn't have to worry about those things, and since he generally picked up such garments at 35 to 50 percent of the regular cost, he could offer our customers real bargains. We could sell $18 slacks for $8, and the manufacturers knew their branded merchandise would be "buried" in small towns like Scottsville, far from their department store clients.

My dad would contract for irregulars with eminent manufacturers such as Blue Bell, which makes Wrangler jeans, and with the companies that manufactured clothing for Sears or J. C. Penney. Then, when they wanted to close out a line at the end of the season, they'd come to him first and he'd get a great price on that too. By the seventies, irregulars and closeouts accounted for 60 percent of the merchandise sold in DG stores. The rest was first-quality apparel, housewares, shoes, and health and beauty aids. He was completely opportunistic when it came to inventory, and this kind of buying was one of the reasons we were so successful.

In fact, through the years my dad developed a reputation for being a genius as a buyer, in particular for looking at something and knowing what it could bring. Actually, you're a genius if it sells at the price you put on it. On the other hand, who's to say it wouldn't have sold just as well at a higher price? When you have a boss like Cal Turner, loved by everyone, you're going to make him a genius in memory. The truth is that for all practical purposes he was really good. He knew when he was pretty much the only remaining outlet for something a manufacturer had and he'd negotiate harder in those instances. He knew where he could price something given his cost, and if it didn't sell well, he'd lower the price further.

He had a hands-on relationship with warehouse operations as well, and he spent a lot of time going up and down the aisles. He would say, "Send this to the Guntersville, Alabama, store," or "The price isn't right on this—let's change it."

His approach was not going to mix well with computers, and he resisted them from the first time he was introduced to the earliest versions. He wasn't crazy about machinery of any kind. When the company opened Nashville store No. 4, Walter Gupton bought six cash registers for $900 without telling my dad, who reacted so badly that Walter thought surely he'd be fired. My dad thought the dollar store business was so simple—especially when you had even-dollar price points—you didn't need sophisticated equipment that would "cost more than it comes to." We'd taken a catch-as-catch-can approach to cash registers from the start, and as far as my dad was concerned, the more basic the better. He didn't want to pay for a register that did anything more than add numbers.

Computers were a bone of contention between my dad and me as well. When I started working for the company, I looked at ways we might improve pretty much every aspect of the business, and George Peterson, the IBM salesman from Bowling Green, convinced me in 1971 that we ought to have computers for inventory control. He and I went into my dad's office to talk about it. My dad said, "Say I go to a manufacturer and buy all that he has. If your computer tells me I've made a good buy, I can't take any action because there's no more to buy. If it tells me I've made a bad buy, I'm going to want to throw the thing out the window. So what use is that to me?"

As George walked out of my dad's office, he looked over all those bookkeepers with their adding machines and had an "aha" moment.

"Look at all these women pounding calculators," he said. He began talking about the "accounting machines" we could bring in to handle all those calculations. Finally, my dad agreed and we were able to buy IBM System/3 computers with punch cards. Given his aversion to the word *computers*, he and I always called them "accounting machines."

My dad was right about the fact that computers didn't make sense for the way he ran the business, but we had them now, and that was a step forward that fulfilled that prophecy—he wasn't going to be running things as he had been. A lot of things were going to change, and that was going to create problems.

Computers didn't change my dad's approach to the tasks he

treasured most. Since the first days of the company, he had gone through the manually prepared reports on every store. When we started using computers, he went through printed reports, and when he got his own computer, all he ever did with it was pull up store reports. For the rest of his career, he remained passionate in his dislike of computers!

True to form, his office looked like the sanctuary of somebody resisting change. He had papers everywhere, both those reports and notes he'd written to himself. He had a big Swedish chair with an ottoman that served almost as a recliner. The credenza behind his desk was loaded with photographs and memorabilia. He had two couches that faced each other—one of which he used for the occasional nap. On the wall behind that one hung an old-fashioned rug that depicted a Saint Bernard dog.

Walking in, you might see him on the phone, buying merchandise, or talking business with somebody, but odds are he was going through those reports. He read every one every week, circling things that caught his eye and making notes to district managers, who received reports with attached notes on problem stores in their district. He might circle the utilities and write, "Please stop heating the out-of-doors." He'd see an amount listed as "stripping and waxing the floor" and write, "In the old days, we did this ourselves." He might circle payroll and write, "Looks like enough for a whole district."

The district managers referred to those missives as "love letters." They definitely had personality, and my dad would show me the choice ones—he'd be so proud of some remark he'd made and what he'd caught in the report that he'd want me to see it before he mailed it.

Now and then he'd call me in and I'd squirm as he went over his "bitch list." He was a man who processed and vented his anger immediately. You knew exactly where you stood and exactly where *he* stood on any point. He generally thought he was right, and he had a world of experience, which he felt deserved to be respected, although it was okay to stand up to him. In fact, he hated spineless yes-men. Most likely he would win or there would be a standoff, but there were times, rare though they were, when he would lose one. It happened now and then with me, and when he had clearly lost, as he did once when we disagreed on pricing greeting cards, he would acknowledge it.

My dad liked to see people in motion. "Don't ever hire someone who doesn't walk fast," he would say. Once, as he was practically running through the warehouse, he saw Delbert Cushenberry, the warehouse supervisor, leaning against the shaft of our old, slow-motion freight elevator, pressing the button. It was a peculiarity of this elevator that you had to push the button the entire time it was moving or it would stop. Daddy knew that, but his intensity was such that the sight of Cush, who was never in much of a hurry, just standing there with his finger on the button got to him.

"Cush, what are you doing?" he said.

"Mr. Turner," he said, "I'm moving the elevator up to the second floor. I've got to hold this button in."

My dad said, "Well, shuffle your feet while you're doing it!"

He also used to complain about meetings. If someone said, "We need to sit down and talk about that," he'd say, "No, we don't. The trouble with this company is how long our meetings are. We need to have stand-up meetings." He liked people to keep their comments brief and to the point, although he exempted himself from that prescription.

It was like that with golf too. My dad would play a round now and then, but he wasn't a fan of other executives who did. "I'm not going to hire anybody who plays golf," he'd say to Howard Johnson, one of our executives—often while they were playing a round.

"Son," he said to me, "look out if you're about to hire somebody who plays golf. It takes too much time. And be careful if you're about to hire somebody who fishes. *That* takes too much time. And, son, if you ever hire anybody who does both, I will fire you."

My dad was a cut-to-the-chase kind of guy. He would make decisions as an entrepreneur and announce them, but he couldn't explain how he got there, even to his son. I spent a lot of time trying to explore the why of his what. I would ask him to interpret something for me and he'd struggle, unable to tell me why he thought this or did that or decided the other. It could be anything from a pricing decision, to why he liked women's clothing to the right of the front door and men's to the left. Sometimes when I said, "Daddy, tell me why you decided that," he would say, "Well, I don't know. It just seemed right."

I could follow up all I wanted, but we could never quite get it pinned down.

There was a time when his logic left me completely in the dark. It happened in 1971, as we were about to issue another public offering of stock, reducing the family's ownership of the company from 73 to 45 percent. I was actually kind of emotional about having that much of the company gone from the family. J. C. Bradford & Co. and White, Weld & Co. were the underwriters, and I was in charge of the process. Everything was moving along nicely until one Monday morning my dad walked into my office and said, "Tell Luke Simons [of J. C. Bradford] the deal is off."

"Why is the deal off, Daddy?" I said.

"I can't tell you," he said.

"There has to be a reason."

"Yes, there is."

"And you can't tell me?"

"No," he said, "I can't tell you, but the deal's off."

When I called Luke, he asked if he could drive up from Nashville to talk to my father, and I told him it would be a wasted trip, which it turned out to be. My dad wouldn't tell him either.

Ten days later, my dad came back into my office.

"Call Luke and tell him the deal's back on," he said.

"Why is the deal back on?" I said.

"I can't tell you," he said.

We went forward again, and when everything was lined up, I prepared to go to Chicago for the settlement. The deal included about $9 million for my dad, who said, "Son, when you go to get my money from this sale of stock, I want you to bring it back in a cashier's check. Don't wire it."

So I went and they put the check in an envelope and I stapled it to the inside of my jacket pocket. Now, my dad had also told me to go to Marshall Field's while I was there and pick something for him to give my mother for her birthday. "Buy her some nice lingerie or something," he said.

So I walked in to Marshall Field's, listing a little to starboard because of that envelope, which sat pretty heavily there in my coat pocket. I went into the ladies' department, which had a freestanding display enclosed in glass so you could walk all around it. It held a mannequin wearing a beautiful robe and gown. I was admiring it when this rather matronly clerk came up to me and said, "May I help you?"

I said, "I think I would like to buy that."

"No, you don't," she whispered.

"What do you mean, 'No, I don't'?"

She looked at me. "That," she said in a stage whisper, "is over six hundred dollars."

"Well, then," I said with an internal chuckle, "just show me something else."

If the devil had gotten into me, I might have reached into my pocket and said, "I wonder if you could cash this for me." The way it was, she never, ever knew, and the incident told me that it's never wise to underestimate your customer.

It was a good twenty years before I found out why my dad was being so mysterious.

9

❦

Filling the Suit

In 1972, I was the executive vice president of a $60-million-a-year business with 500 stores. Our typical store had 3,500 square feet of selling space and did $150,000 a year in sales, in a rural area with a population under 10,000. Going back to the days when I was a part-time employee in the warehouse and in the store as a teenager, I had been with the company for more than twenty years. I was thirty-two years old, with a wife and a son, Calister III, who'd been born in 1971. My development, as a leader and as a man, was still a work in progress.

My political history, at least in the early years, was tied to my parents. My mother's family included quite a few politicians, some of them prominent, all of them Democrats, and a lot of the talk at family events was political. My dad was just the opposite. He never talked about politics. He felt that a businessman ought to keep his mouth shut about such things—as Michael Jordan said many years later when asked why he wasn't politically active, "Republicans buy sneakers too." My dad was a Republican, but in this case, he wanted neither Republicans nor Democrats to have a reason not to shop in his stores.

I registered to vote at eighteen in 1958—Kentucky was one of the first states to lower the voting age to eighteen, doing so in 1955—as a Democrat. If you were voting in my part of Kentucky—and in much of the South—the Democratic primary was where the action was, because the Democrat was, more than likely, going to win the general election.

I had believed from the time I was young that the government ought to do everything possible to help the less fortunate. My year-and-a-half in Scotland, though, had a big effect on my outlook. Many of the people around Thurso lived in socialized housing—there was socialized everything, really—and it seemed to me that it didn't work. Shopkeepers, for instance, weren't motivated to open their shops long enough to get a lot of business. Clearly, the government had its hand in too much of the economy, and it was obvious that the system was not designed to encourage enterprise.

Then, when I got back home, I watched Lyndon Johnson's determination to fight a war in Vietnam while simultaneously launching a Great Society, which seemed to me to be a movement toward the very society that wasn't working very well in Great Britain. Not long afterward, I changed my registration, becoming what I called "an LBJ Republican," meaning he had driven me to the GOP.

One thing I appreciated about Scotland was their dress. They may not have opened for business often enough to suit me, but they always seemed to be dressed well for business. I liked that. In my early years of leading the company, I felt that I needed to dress like the boss. That was a part of the Turner mentality that may well have come to my dad through the Goad side of the family. The Goads were sharp dressers and one, Frank Goad Clement, who was Tennessee's governor for ten years in the 1950s and '60s, once told a story about showing up in a small town looking like a million dollars and meeting a man who beamed and said, "Look, you are my governor, and when you show up, I want you to be dressed well and be in the biggest Cadillac they make." Both my parents were sharp dressers. My dad was generally in a suit. He felt it was a way to show respect to the people you were dealing with. My mother wore a hat and gloves to church and changed her attire seasonally with the coming each year of the Kentucky Derby and Labor Day—and their example made me conscious of dress all my life. We would go into Nashville to shop at the Castner-Knott, Harvey's, and Cain Sloan department stores when I was a kid. I remember being the only one of my friends to wear knickers—corduroy knickers, no less, which made noise when I walked. My parents must have thought they were stylish. I remember my joy in receiving my first yellow cashmere sweater, a Christmas present from my mother, and at fifteen or sixteen, a sharp-looking pale blue dinner jacket, my first, for a dance.

In my late twenties, while I was still single, I was appearance-conscious enough that I decided to get hair transplants. I traveled regularly to New Orleans for the procedures, and before I left on one of those trips, I decided to get the Lowrey organ I had at home repaired.

"Earline," I said to my secretary, "while I'm gone, I want you to get the Lowrey people to come from Bowling Green and fix the wow-wow on my organ."

She paused and cleared her throat.

"Well...if you ever get hair growing on your head and your wow-wow working, you'll be something, won't you?"

There was always a lot of color and a little flair to the way I dressed—still is—but it was always business dress. It wasn't until very late in my career that I was willing to let Dollar General's office staff adopt casual dress on Fridays. I'd been under pressure to do so, and then one Father's Day, Margaret and my son, Cal, gave me a lot of casual clothes, so I got the hint and finally loosened up. I did find that it was harder to combine colors and patterns in putting together a casual outfit than it was to don a shirt, tie, and coat.

Wearing the suit was one thing. Filling it was another. From day one, my dad wanted me to share the number one role, and for twelve-and-a-half years I carried an awesome sense of the weight of that position, always aware that I had the responsibility of being number one but not the full authority—that was something I shared with my father. But I was going to have to amass knowledge as though the responsibility were solely mine.

Paradoxically, I was empowered by my dad's inability to teach. Throughout my professional life, I ran across people like him who had grassroots creativity but didn't know how to share it. I had to figure out how to draw the lessons from each person and situation even when those lessons were subtle or not articulated. I had to take charge of my own learning. That positioned me to learn more from life and others than if my dad had simply declared principles to me. In fact, I have trouble with principles. They feel like something that comes from on high that you accept without questioning. Rather, there should be propositions arising from individual experience. I learned that principles aren't completely transportable from my life to yours. I can't profess to have the truth to declare from on high, because I don't. I have the lessons of my experience.

Consequently, I was sometimes suspicious of management paradigms. "Management by objectives" was king when I started, but I realized early on that I wanted more than just an objective. "Do this" was not enough for me. I was interested in the people side of getting things done. As a would-be pastor disguised as a businessman, I wanted heart, not just objectives. I wanted a different kind of leadership agenda.

My observation of how things were done in the early days made me conclude that "organized chaos" was the apt description of our company. Our warehousing and distribution system was a case in point. Goods came in from manufacturers, then went back out to the stores. Orders came in to different departments with no real coordination. A truck driver headed for, say, the store in Jackson, Tennessee, would go from department to department in the warehouses and say, "Have you got anything for Jackson?" If that store's merchandise didn't fill the truck, he'd be assigned another store in the area or on the way. He'd go around again. "Have you got anything for Dickson?" He'd fill the truck and drive off.

I remember walking through the warehouses with David Wilds of J. C. Bradford. David had brought a potential investor to look at the company. The three of us were in the "Cush" warehouse, named for its slow-talking manager, Delbert Cushenberry, and we had come to the section where we kept our Blue Bell stock—their irregulars and closeouts on jeans. We had them piled up everywhere. My dad liked them to be sent to stores bundled by the dozen in a mix of colors and sizes. That way, we could ask the stores, "How many dozen do you think you need of the five-dollar jeans?" and we'd send them whatever mix we came up with. We did the same thing with blouses.

David and this investor looked at what amounted to almost an entire warehouse of jeans, and David said, "Cal, how do you know where anything is?"

"Cush!" I yelled. "Men's, thirty-two-inch waist!"

"Well," he said, "I think there's some over there," and he walked over, and sure enough, there were some. It was low-tech but it seemed to work.

When the fellow in charge of store operations—we had imported him from another company—left us after a year on the job, I sat with him for an exit interview.

"Cal Jr.," he said, "do you realize we have six different warehouses which independently ship to stores with no coordination? There is nobody in charge of warehousing in this company!"

He didn't say "distribution." He said, "warehousing." And after that interview, I thought, *Yes, somebody should be in charge of warehousing*, so we took that step, somewhere in the mid-seventies, as we worked to tweak our seat-of-the-pants process. By 1976, we had more than 2,000 stockholders in forty-five states and five countries. We had 2,500 employees, and our sales were at $109 million, up from

$26 million a decade earlier. We were the fourteenth largest company in Kentucky in terms of net sales, and in the top twenty-five in terms of assets. We were the only one headquartered outside a major metropolitan area—thirty of the top forty were headquartered in Louisville—and I'm convinced our small-town roots and continued presence in Scottsville helped us to be in touch with our customers.

One of our annual reports put it like this: "We've always lived in small towns, always done business in small towns, and we're their kind of people. Small-town people work harder for their money and often have less of it to spend, so they're more careful and practical about how they spend it. They judge quality by the garment, not the label, and they know a work shirt with a thread pattern flaw will last just as long as first line merchandise even if it only costs half as much. They don't mind shopping where there's no carpeting, indirect lighting or soft music, because they know it's the customer who pays for those luxuries.

"We're in Scottsville, Kentucky, with our corporate headquarters and warehouses for many of the same kind of reasons. We can do business less expensively, with better help, and with more pleasant surroundings than our big-city competitors. We're country folks and we intend to stay that way, even though we think we're doing a big-city job of merchandising."

It was a mind-set I watched and tried to absorb, but there were still lessons I needed to learn. It took my brother, Steve, to teach me one of them.

Steve, who graduated from Vanderbilt in 1969 and spent a couple of years in the Army, had come into the business in the early seventies as a buyer. He had worked in stores and in the warehouse as a teenager, too, so that seemed the right first placement of him in the company.

There aren't many things I would do over, but given the chance, I might react differently to my brother's choice of career. Growing up, he would say, "Cal Jr., I wish you'd go on and decide what you want to do so I'll know what I'm not going to do. I don't want you to be my boss." He wanted to be a lawyer at one point, but my dad over-ruled that. "No," he told Steve, "I want you to be productive." Steve had married and started a family while at Vanderbilt, and after the Army he decided to join the company. He and I should have had a real heart-to-heart about how it would be with one brother working for another. I should have talked to my dad about it as well. I wasn't insightful enough to understand it at the time, but Steve was coming in under two shadows. I only came in under one—my father's. Steve had mine as well. I was already established in the business. My dad made sure I was accepted and I was doing things he wasn't doing. Steve was also a Turner in need of establishing his own identity.

I had started out learning how to open a store from scratch and then how to rent store buildings at $1 per square foot. My dad didn't want me in his merchandising playhouse so I just watched him and observed how he went about it, without playing a role. He was the one functioning entity in merchandising. There was so much else in the company I needed to sink my teeth into. But I wasn't a buyer, so that was somewhere Steve could serve the company separate from me. My dad was by then willing to bring another son into the part of the business that was closest to his heart. That part of retailing had the further advantage of being a more sociable area. If there is a party component to retailing, it would be in merchandising, in schmoozing and being schmoozed by the salesmen.

But having both my dad and Steve in that part of the business set the stage for a lot of father-son difficulty because they didn't think or act alike. Steve did respect my dad as a merchant, but they would inevitably wind up at odds over one thing or another.

At one point I needed some more management bodies to take to a meeting with financial analysts.

"Steve," I said, "I want you to go with me to represent management,

10

❧

Scottsville Divided:
The Teamsters Strike

Late in the summer of 1976, the Teamsters Union launched an effort to organize our truck drivers and warehouse employees. The Teamsters had been founded in 1903 and had classically represented drivers and warehouse workers, although they had since expanded into other job types. We had maybe twenty drivers and a fleet of two dozen tractors and four dozen trailers carrying merchandise from the warehouses in Scottsville—our only distribution location—to stores that stretched from Delaware to Oklahoma and from Indiana to Florida.

We had faced a number of organizing efforts by unions dating back to the one that so upset my dad when I was in the Navy. He was sick about all of them. My dad was passionate and outspoken about his opposition to unions; he would get red in the face at the very mention of them.

I remember that during one attempt to organize J. L. Turner and Son employees, a bookkeeper named Barbara invited two other bookkeepers to join her for lunch with a union organizer. My dad found out about it and saw to it that she was fired by five o'clock that afternoon. She called him at home and I happened to be there. I knew what we as a company could and couldn't say to employees at times like this—you couldn't threaten or fire employees for getting information about unions—and I had tried to explain all that to my dad. I stood by the phone, hoping for the best as they began talking.

"Mr. Turner," she said, "I want to know why I was fired from J. L. Turner and Son."

"Well, Barbara," he said, "I can't discuss that with you until Mr. Craddock [who was in charge of the bookkeepers] and I can sit down together and talk about it."

Yes! I thought. *He's aced it.* Now if I could just get him off the phone.

"However," he said—and I knew something bad was coming—"I think everyone should know that we don't intend to have any union sympathizers working for J. L. Turner and Son."

He had just blown it, of course. From then on, at every single hearing we had before the National Labor Relations Board, usually involving a grievance filed during an organizing drive, that quote from Cal Sr. was introduced and placed in the record, often without any relevance to the case at hand.

The toughness on our side—going back to the earlier organizational effort, when my dad helped make it harder on union sympathizers to get bank loans—will certainly raise eyebrows given present-day sensibilities, but in those days labor relations, like race relations, were much different. Union organizers played hardball, as did those who opposed them. One had only to look to the coal mines of Kentucky and West Virginia and their decades of sometimes deadly strife to know that. There was genuine horror in many towns, including Scottsville, at the prospect of union activity. In the face of my dad's complete hatred of the unions and his inability to disguise it or remain silent, I was the one who had to remain measured and calm, and I oversaw the company's handling of the matter. Given that we were a family business in a small town, the fight gave me the first taste of hell in my career.

We had managed our own transportation since the beginning, when Leo Allen was hauling merchandise in his own cattle truck. In 1957, the company invested in two trucks of its own and Leo started driving one of them. Through the years, we bought trucks and trailers one or two at a time from various sources, and we drove them hard. We figured it was better to pay the maintenance bills and keep trucks on the road as long as we could rather than trade them in too often. Leo, for instance, put a quarter of a million miles on each of five new trucks through 1973. In those one-and-a-quarter-million miles, by the way, he was involved in only two accidents, and the insurance company ruled that neither was his fault.

The company had always been more union-vulnerable with the drivers than with any other group of employees. They traveled. They came in contact with drivers from all over the country and knew they were paid less than many of their counterparts. On the other hand, our truck drivers made more money than our warehouse workers, and that was its own problem. There was always going to be some tension there, union or no union. At one point, well over two years before this union drive began, we had decided we could kill several birds with one stone by outsourcing our transportation. We could let someone else be responsible for the drivers' wages and benefits. So we petitioned the Interstate Commerce Commission for permission to bring in outside contractors. But then, as with so many other things, the idea sat on the shelf.

The election to determine whether our drivers would choose representation by the Teamsters for the purpose of collective bargaining with the company came, and the drivers voted the Teamsters in. Meanwhile, the union was still talking to the warehouse workers, who had their own vote scheduled thirty days later. My dad was beside himself. We had to do something.

We had a Kentucky lawyer advising us during the run-up to the drivers' vote. Now we decided we needed more horsepower, and we

brought in an Atlanta law firm. One of their lawyers led our negotiations concerning the truckers' contract and another ran our
campaign against the Teamsters regarding the warehouse workers'
pending vote.

We thought it was a shame that the drivers had voted in the
union. As far as we were concerned, they had a good thing going
since we cared more about their welfare than did the Teamsters, who
were looking for dues money and for a checkoff system requiring that
all drivers be unionized, willingly or not. We thought that agreeing to
those things would have been a betrayal of the very drivers the union
was claiming to represent. Still, we understood human nature well
enough to know that peer pressure can sway everyone. We thought
they had been locked into a narrow and short-term self-interest by a
union that had issues like their pay well down its list of concerns.

Our official position in negotiating with the drivers was that we
couldn't agree to the Teamsters' demands. We had the concerns of
several constituencies to think about. We had to think about customers, employees, including the drivers, and Dollar General itself.
There was a huge gap between what we, as a company based in Scottsville, Kentucky, could pay and what they were demanding. It would
upset the entire cost structure of the company. The whole model of
low-cost retailing that gave low everyday prices to the customer and
allowed us to succeed in the first place was in jeopardy. Raising their
pay and benefits that much would lead to similar demands from our
warehouse workers and our store employees. We viewed fighting
those demands as something we had to do.

Given the election results, there was nothing we could do about
the drivers except to negotiate, but we could certainly work on the
warehouse employees. We brought in the department heads and gave
them common-sense talking points to take back to their workers.

"We have a direct relationship with you now," we told our employees through them. "The union is a third party. Any promise they

make to you is something *we* have to fulfill, so they're not really in a position to make those promises. Can you imagine any successful marriage that invited a third party in to run interference? Can you imagine that making for better communication or a better marriage?"

Meanwhile, our law firm went into high gear. It was an interesting dynamic to see them work both fronts of this conflict while trying to create the perception that those were separate and unrelated endeavors. It was all high-stakes gamesmanship with a lot of grandstanding.

It was also very serious. The lawyer we had engaged in the election campaign said, "We're not going to lose. The closest I've ever come to losing an election, there was a guy in charge of the plant who was really liked by everybody. He was in charge of our campaign, which was going badly. He had a new car and we told him it was going to be smashed in that night at his house. 'Don't go out, don't do anything,' we told him. 'Just drive it in to work tomorrow and park it in your regular parking place.'"

He told me the workers were so incensed at what had been done to the boss's car that they voted the union down.

That's using a falsely created perception to help you win a union election, and to my mind it's outside the rulebook. I hated to think of a law firm engaging in that kind of thing, and fortunately, so far we hadn't had to take that route. Still, I felt really bad about observing the union negotiate for itself and not for employees, and we took a hard line, particularly in regards to the checkoff system, whereby all employees were required to belong to the union and the company would be automatically collecting dues and sending them to the union. In response, the union wanted to take the drivers out on strike, but held off because they knew a strike would erode their support among the warehouse workers. They knew it was in their interest to wait for the warehouse vote.

As that election neared, we took the advice of our law firm and divided paychecks in two. The department head would hand out checks that represented each worker's pay minus what he or she would be paying the union in dues. "That's what you'll take home if you vote this union in," they said. Then they handed out the check that represented the union dues. "This will be going to the union," they said, "but don't forget it is really your pay and the money does come from us."

That little bit of drama was perfectly legal, and we did attempt to stay inside the lines, something we were concerned the union might not do.

I called Bill Coble of Coble Systems, a transportation company in Nashville. Bill and I had been talking for a long time about a truck leasing deal, although we'd never been able to agree on a price. Besides solving our Teamsters problem, a deal with Coble would place the responsibility for trucks, drivers, fuel, and insurance with someone else. Now we needed to get serious about our negotiations.

Bill told me he'd talk with his father and brother and his department heads and get back to me. I found out later that his department heads considered the possible danger and all said, "No, we don't want to do this." Bill liked challenges, but he still hadn't made up his mind. He went into work that next morning and told his secretary, "Cal is going to call me at ten. Let me know when he's on the phone." Finally, he decided to flip a coin—a half-dollar.

If it comes up heads, he thought, *I'm going to tell him we're not going to do it.* It came up heads and he said, "The hell with the coin. I'm going to do it anyhow."

Bill told me he'd get the pricing together and come to see me. He worked day and night for two or three days and then came to my office with a thick proposal. He sat down at my desk and started talking. I saw him look over my shoulder and he started laughing.

"You've seen my sign," I said. It said, in foot-high letters, *Hasten*

Thy Story. I told him I'd take the proposal home and meet him at eight o'clock the next morning. It took some negotiating, but we reached an agreement. It was far more lucrative for them than we'd have liked under ordinary circumstances, but we were desperate to get merchandise to our stores and his company was ready to do battle.

We won the election in the warehouse—the workers voted down the union—and that's when the fireworks started. The Teamsters called a strike of the drivers and set up a picket line in an attempt to intimidate the warehouse workers. That shut down our warehouses and, since the only ones we had were in Scottsville, effectively shut down the company.

Some people crossed the picket line, braving the taunts and threats of the strikers; some didn't. One who did was Toncie Towe, who was eighty years old. The first day she reached the line, one of the picketers told her to turn around and go home.

"Look here," she said. "If the Turners are nice enough to give an old lady a job, she's going to come to work. Get out of my way!"

She revved her motor and they did.

Given the circumstances, we went ahead with our plan to divest the company of its in-house transportation. Dad and I realized that in the long run outsourcing was going to be the way to handle our shipping. We contacted the ICC and the application we had submitted years earlier became our emergency authorization to bring in outside contractors.

The situation in Scottsville got more and more tense as people took either the union's side or the Turners'. We had a brand-new minister at the Methodist church and I remember his coming to me and asking about the company and the strike. I could tell by his questions that he hadn't decided whether he was going to side with the drivers or with us.

One of the strikers said at one point that the problem with the company was that the wrong Turner boy was running it. Seven years younger than I was, Steve was almost of a different generation. He was a hail-fellow-well-met kind of guy, someone everyone liked and could identify with. I was the straight arrow—always had been—and he was socially inclined with quick wit and the gift of gab. I think part of it was that he took on that kind of persona in order to be his own person, as that was true to his nature. If anything, I may have been too serious. My dad was what he'd always been—sort of the god of the company. Each Turner son formed his company image relative to that reality. Sometimes my role was defined by default. If someone working for Steve had to be fired, I would sometimes have to do it, since he didn't want to any more than my dad did. It seemed at times I was the only Turner who fired anybody. It was a skill I learned on the job, although it was never something I relished. I once tried to fire somebody and just couldn't bring myself to do it on the first attempt. He came to work the next day and I had to do it again. I called him back in and I said, "You know, yesterday I intended to fire you, but I just couldn't do it. So that's what I'm doing today."

Going back to my days in the military and perhaps before, I had a tendency to be too rigid, but that's not the same as being decisive, and clearly this was a time for decisiveness. We had to get our merchandise moving. We had arranged for a firm in Nashville to send armed guards to provide security at the warehouses and ride with the Coble truckers. We were going to send the first trucks out Sunday, and late Friday afternoon I decided I'd better call to make sure everything was set. I was driving toward Kentucky, on I-65 near Goodlettsville, Tennessee, and I pulled off the interstate. I was standing in a phone booth when I reached my contact at the security company, who told me the deal was off. Never will I forget the cold fear that ran through me; immediately, I called our lead lawyer in Atlanta and told him we needed security fast. He told me he'd worked with the Wackenhut security firm on other union matters and that he'd see what he could do. He reached their headquarters in Miami and they had a crew in Scottsville the next morning, helping us to mobilize.

Sure enough, once those trucks started rolling, everything escalated. We put a guard in the passenger seat in every truck and sent a car with a driver and an armed guard in front of and behind every truck. The picketers were loud and confrontational, but the trucks went through. During the first few days, there were tires shot out and one of the guards got excited and blew a hole through the roof of a cab. A car with its license plate covered pulled alongside one of our tractor-trailers on the highway and unloaded a pistol into the cab. Miraculously, no one was hurt. In Nashville, someone blew up a trailer parked in one of Coble's lots. We had store windows bashed in and there was other mischief.

Finally, it hit home. I was company spokesman, the one the area's newspapers and TV stations talked to. I was the visible face of the company. I went to bed one Saturday night after taking some cold medicine, and around 2:00 a.m., I woke to a couple of loud retorts. I remember thinking, "That sounds like gunshots," but I was groggy and went back to sleep. The next afternoon, Calister and I were at a friend's home and I got a call from Margaret, who had gone into the living room and found bullet holes in our front door. We called the police and they came to investigate.

About a week later, Steve came into my office to tell our father and me that a manufacturer's rep said his secretary had heard that there was a kidnapping contract on five-year-old Calister. It was an unbelievably frightening thing for us to hear. We immediately made provisions for Wackenhut to provide an armed guard to be near my son twenty-four hours a day. Oddly enough, as worried as we were, it was great for Calister, because he had somebody he could play with, someone on whose shoulders he could ride. He actually enjoyed it.

Our newspaper carrier wasn't nearly as enthusiastic. He would drive down our street and pull far enough into the drive that he could toss the Louisville *Courier-Journal* close to the door, then turn around and drive off. He drove up one morning only to have two Wackenhut guards emerge from the bushes and accost him.

"Mr. Turner," he said in the note he left with the newspaper that morning, "I will not be delivering your paper again until the strike is over."

For a few nights, we slept in the basement of my parents' home. It was concrete, so it was the safest place available to us.

Not long afterward, one of our executives who had been through situations like this elsewhere urged us to up the ante.

"Cal Jr.," he said to me one day, "you're playing by the rules and it isn't working. You're losing. They've shot into your home, there's a kidnapping contract on Calister, they've shot into employees' homes and bashed in store windows. It's time for us to show them that they can bleed too. This doesn't need to be traced to you. All you have to do is blink your eyes and I'll take care of it."

I can tell you that you don't really understand temptation until you experience it like this. I knew it would be wrong to go down that road, but I don't want to claim that it was pure virtue that made me tell him "no." I knew what was right, but I also knew what was practical. Saying "yes" would make a bad situation worse. Any violence to come shouldn't be coming from our side.

"I'm telling you specifically that we are not going to do that," I said. "I don't want you to think you saw me nod or blink. We're not doing it."

As it was, there was probably as much tension in that little town of 4,000 as there had ever been or would ever be again. There were four times as many Wackenhut guards in Scottsville as there were city policemen. The atmosphere was just awful. And to this day, I am security conscious, with a part of me fully in tune with the mob types who sit with their backs to the wall, always aware of who is coming and going.

Scottsville's size also meant that interconnections were many and interesting. At one point, after a session in which one of our lawyers, Joe Bill Campbell, had counseled our witnesses in preparation for a hearing about an injunction related to the strike, Steve, Joe Bill, and I were talking.

"Joe Bill," I said, "do you have any advice for Steve or me?"

"No," he said. Then he paused for a moment. "Oh, just one thing. Please don't refer to the judge as Uncle Frank."

Uncle Frank Goad, my mother's brother, was by then the circuit judge, and he saw no reason to recuse himself. He did handle himself well. During one hearing, he said, "Well, everybody's here. Union, management, we're all in the room. We have just had a bomb threat, but nobody's going to leave this room for the next two hours. We're going to stay right here." Which is what we did.

Somehow, amid all of this, you could sense the tide beginning to shift from the Teamsters toward the Turners. Maybe it was that the percentage of townspeople who'd joined the union was so small. Maybe it was all the mischief that had gone on. In any case, opinion was moving our way, and I'm convinced that turning down our executive's offer was the wisest thing I could have done. If I had given him the go-ahead, it would really have exacerbated an already explosive situation.

Rulings started coming our way as well. The NLRB, which I felt was prejudiced in favor of unions, nevertheless ruled against the Teamsters. Then a court ruled in a lawsuit filed by the union that the company was within its rights to employ outsiders to do its hauling because it had applied for authority to do so long before the strike—there was no apparent connection between the union's organization drive and the company's application for outside transportation.

In the face of those rulings, and amid unusually cold October weather, the picketing stopped. Those in-house trucking jobs were gone for good. That was one of the saddest parts of the situation.

The people who'd lost those jobs were from Scottsville and Allen County. A lot of them had been good company men. Some of them eventually started speaking to me again, but some never did. I hated it. This was a company that had been like family in a town that supported workers and management alike. We still handed out bonuses and boxes of candy to each warehouse employee at our annual Christmas party, yet the strike had injected a dose of harsh reality into all of it.

Coble handled our trucking for many years, through expansions into other warehouses around the South as the company entered yet another growth phase. We never again had in-house transportation.

As sort of a postscript, five or six years later, an agent of the Bureau of Alcohol, Tobacco and Firearms was in my office. He said, "Oh, by the way, I heard your name mentioned in the pen last week."

"What do you mean?" I said.

"Well, I was talking with the inmate who had the contract to kidnap your son."

Cold fear went all over me. I had done what had to be done in order to protect young Calister, but the fact that somebody was actually planning to kidnap him didn't sink in until that moment. I have always been somewhat naïve, and have even cherished that naïveté, but this, as the last bit of fallout from a traumatic time in company history, showed me how the real world can shatter rose-colored glasses.

11

✎

Expansion: Breaking the Commandments

I became company president in 1977, and the conversation that kicked off the process, like the one that followed that card game blowup years earlier, took place through a closed door as my dad sat on the john. Sometimes it was easier for us to reveal what we were really thinking when we couldn't see each other.

"Son," he said, "I have decided it's time for you to become president so I can be chairman for a long time!"

I knew he was referring to his age. His attitude was that although I could run the company forever as executive vice president, maybe it was time to change titles and let him wear "chairman," a new position for us, from here on out. He was making it sound as if he were doing it for himself, when we both knew he was doing it for me.

"So, I want you and Rod Wenz [who was still running our public relations from Louisville] to decide the right time to do it," he said.

"Okay."

The idea just sat there until three months later, when an editor for *Fortune* named Eleanor Tracy came to Scottsville with an assistant and a photographer to do a story for the magazine. My dad and I, along with Steve and a couple of other senior managers, took her outside of town to Ethel Foster's Home Cooking, where you sit at a table with a red and white checkerboard tablecloth and pass homemade vegetables, ham, fried chicken, and corn bread. Afterward, we pushed back from the table and Eleanor turned to my dad and said, "So, Mr. Turner, when is Cal Jr. becoming president?"

"Well, I don't know," he said. "Cal Jr., when do you want to be president?"

Eleanor got the most perplexed expression on her face. I said, "Eleanor, is that what this article is about?"

"Well," she said, "I heard from Rod Wenz that you were becoming president."

"Do you have a deadline for the article?" I asked her.

She told us the date when it was due to hit the stands.

"Okay, I'll be president by then," I told her, and I was.

Once the announcement was made, someone from *People* magazine called and said, "We'll do a story on Mr. Turner if you'll tell us how much he was worth before becoming president and how much he's worth now that he is." We declined.

I went from executive vice president to president and my dad went from president to chairman. Not long afterward, a reporter for the *Louisville Times* asked who was now CEO. I said, "I am, until my dad decides he wants to be for a while, and then he is, until he gets tired of it. Then I pick it back up again." It was just the kind of truth a newspaper doesn't know what to do with, so it didn't make the story.

At first, the word *president* kind of caught in my throat. It scared me. I had moved from boss's son to the leader officially responsible for the future of a company.

The challenges and opportunities came hard and fast. I took a look at things like our long-standing practice of self-insuring. We dealt with the occasional fire or flooding ourselves, but by now we were big enough and complex enough that it might not be possible to operate ourselves out of an insurance problem, particularly if things went wrong in several places at once. Meanwhile, as the number of stores grew, the cost of commercial insurance per store fell. We took bids and realized it finally made more sense to buy insurance with high deductibles.

Then there were acquisition opportunities. We were conservative about such things, or so we thought. In those days, we had what amounted to a handful of company commandments:

- Thou shalt not acquire sick companies.
- Thou shalt not own a company plane.
- Thou shalt not deal with a New York or Chicago bank.
- Thou shalt not have more than one warehouse.

We were about to break every one of them.

We resisted acquisitions because it was easier to open and profit from our own stores than to convert other stores to our system, but our principles were about to come face-to-face with back-to-back opportunities that would test them as never before. Each was larger than any previous purchase we'd undertaken.

The first came when United Dollar Stores, a Dumas, Arkansas, retailer, filed under Chapter 11 of the Bankruptcy Act in November 1976, just as our strike was ending. Along with 88 stores, mostly in Arkansas, Louisiana, and Mississippi, UDS had among its assets a 350,000-square-foot warehouse in Dumas and a company plane. We talked to their principal creditor, a bank in Chicago, which agreed to finance the deal at prime rate. Even so, we wouldn't have seriously considered the acquisition if our largest franchisee, the Rankin Co., hadn't gotten into a tight spot financially. Rankin, based in Columbia, Mississippi, consisted of 27 franchised stores, owned by three partners, who paid us a franchise fee, and 149 stores it owned jointly with us. Geographically, UDS and Rankin overlapped quite nicely and the UDS warehouse sat just about in the middle. Taken together, it all made sense.

We bought Rankin with long-term notes, putting no money down. UDS had a book value of $10.5 million and we paid $6.8 million for all but the warehouse, which we were nevertheless able to use rent-free until the merchandise inside, which we *had* bought, was gone. Then we turned around and conducted a bankruptcy sale. We grossed $7.2 million and incurred expenses of $800,000. Our total investment for 88 stores was $400,000. Since we had greatly expanded our area, we decided to keep the plane. Finally, a year later, we purchased the warehouse for $1.5 million, or $4.28 a square foot.

We knew what had happened to both companies. UDS had once operated a successful dollar store chain, but had moved away from that core business, opening discount stores that charged a membership fee. Rankin had raised prices and reduced inventory to counteract high transportation and administration expenses, and had seen its retail sales decline. Their experiences made us even more determined to stick with our simple, conservative business concept, which we thought would restore both to profitability.

Still, we recognized quickly after the acquisitions of UDS and Rankin that we didn't have the executive staff or the battle plan to oversee the vastly bigger company we had become. We had gone from 418 company-owned stores served by 362,000 square feet of warehouse space to 671 stores served by warehouses totaling more than 700,000 square feet. We had a small management team with plenty of rough edges, and it took us two years to absorb the purchase.

As all of this unfolded so early in my presidency, a thought hit me: *Oh, my gosh, I need more training!* It had been nearly a decade since I'd taken the AMA's management course, but I knew it was time to tap into their expertise again. Their "Management Course for Presidents" seemed ideal and I signed up. Early in 1978, I went to Hamilton, New York, and over the course of a week, learned the basics of strategic planning, a formal process by which a senior management team determines where an organization is going and how it's going to get there, settling on the company's mission, strategies, and objectives. If done well, the process empowers team success.

The implementation of strategic planning at Dollar General would eventually change the way we operated. Its principles would guide the process that led to our biggest breakthroughs as a company. In 1978, though, it was just a great idea, something I knew could be useful for us—and something I knew would fail unless I could get my father on board. I needed his endorsement. I thought, *I have to get his attention, and when a farmer has to get the attention of a mule, sometimes the best way to do that is with a plank.* So, I came home after that training meeting, walked into my dad's office, shut the door, and sat down, waiting for him to get off the telephone. When he did, I said, "Daddy, we have a decision to make."

"What's that, son?" he asked me.

"Whether to do strategic planning now or wait until you're dead!"

"What is strategic planning?" he said, looking startled. I knew at that moment I had his attention.

"It's a process where we open this company up to non-Turners and talk honestly about strengths and weaknesses and opportunities and threats, and we decide about our mission and our objectives. It gets everyone on the same page and helps everybody pull together so we can really develop the company."

There was silence for a long moment, and he said, "Well, son, I know that the way I've always run the company is not right for the future. I do not know what the right way is, but I respect you and your ability to figure that out. Mind you, I'm still going to get on my stump from time to time."

"Well, Daddy, I know that some things are a given."

He said, "Now, I will say this to you. I hope you won't create *plan planners* but will have *plan doers*."

Again, I had underestimated my father. The "old boy" understood the guts of things very well. I always knew that my dad was wonderful, and he had just let go of something very big—his hold on the right to manage the process that determined the company's direction. That moment set in motion a profound change in Dollar General.

In the fall of 1978, a few months after I'd gone through the Management Course for Presidents, I went with ten other Dollar General executives back to Hamilton, New York, to undertake the AMA's strategic planning process. We needed to push strategic planning into the culture of our company and that had to be done through senior management. These sessions were designed to get everyone on board.

The DG executives I often referred to as our "renegade rednecks" and I were assigned to Larry Appley's protégé Hank Pattison, one of the AMA's best planning coordinators. He began to lead us through the process of coming up with the plan we would all implement when we got back to Scottsville.

I remember Hank's eyes swimming around as he dealt with us. It was quickly obvious why they put their best facilitator with the Dollar General group. We were a curious amalgam of human talent from an entrepreneurial company where there was no budget and no real planning. In fact, I'm pretty sure there's never been another company that's gone into strategic planning before it's done budgeting. Early on, Hank took advantage of our lack of knowledge about our own company.

"Who is your customer?" he asked, to laughter from this motley group.

"Okay," he said as the snickers subsided, "just tolerate me here. I want everybody to write down, without talking to each other about it, just who your customer is."

We did, and he collected the pieces of paper. Then he wrote our answers, one after the other, on the board at the front of the room. They were all over the place.

"So we don't have agreement here," he said. "Let's try it again. What business are you in?" There was laughter again, but this time it was much more subdued.

He did the same thing with those answers and got the same result. "So you're unclear about the nature of your business," he said. After a couple more of those, it was obvious that what had looked like a team may well have been pulling in different directions because we hadn't shared a single and well-articulated vision. At that point, we were chastened and ready for him to lead us in a discussion of exactly what we were bringing to whom and why. We spent most of those first sessions—two sets of them, about a month apart—focused on questions that basic.

We defined our customers as "deserving, salt-of-the-earth people struggling to make ends meet." That definition helped us to come up with our first mission statement: "To serve better than anyone else does our customer's need for quality basic merchandise at every-day low prices."

The "so what" of a mission statement is, "In light of that, in what direction should we move?" That gives you your strategy. Getting more specific about strategic objectives gives you operating objectives and operational action plans. That's the process we began in Hamilton, although in actuality we were off and running with our immature version of a mission statement.

Our first order of business was to establish clear communication about where we were presently. I had been studying the business and my father, and had considered myself pretty well up to speed. Now it was time to pull the other executives into that and see where we stood in their eyes. I had begun to set the tone with my acknowledgment that, as the boss's son, I was in over my head and needed their help.

"I need your honesty about our strengths and weaknesses," I said at one of our early strategic planning sessions. "I want your ideas about what we can most effectively do next." I wanted to let them know, too, that this was a team effort in every sense, including financial.

"The success we have," I said, "will be shared with everybody."

They knew I was being sincere, and they felt empowered to be honest. There were any number of specific recommendations, but before long, they went straight to what they saw as a fundamental problem in our business. Ron Humphrys, one of our buyers, was the person who nailed the truth for us.

"Well, Cal Jr.," he said, "I'll tell you what's wrong with the company. It's the way you and your father quote your grandfather—'If it's bought right, it's half sold.'"

"Yes," I said, "so what's wrong with that?"

"So, look at all this half-sold inventory we are stuck with! We need to think about the other half—the *selling* part—what the customer *wants*. We push your dad's big deals out to the stores and a lot of times they just sit there. If we're going to have this business grow, we're going to have to stock what the customers want, so that they come in more often and we can serve them better. We now have buyer push. What we need is customer pull."

My dad's buying habits were one of the things that set us apart. By and large, the other retailers studied and copied one another. That's why you could probably go into any department store and find pretty much what was in every other—you still can. They advertise the heck out of being like one another, then try to put just a bit more style, a bit more froufrou, into the presentation, hoping to woo you to this one instead of that one. That froufrou also allows them to mark things up a little higher, getting more from shoppers for the same merchandise. That is perhaps a good retailing example of what happens when you pay more attention to the competition than to the customer.

We were different. We avoided froufrou. We knew it was harder to convince the customer she's getting a bargain if she sees carpeting and a boutique setting. That's part of why our furnishings were so sparse.

"What are the best buys we can find and pass along to our customer?" was my dad's bottom line. We reasoned that lowering the prices would bring more customers in the door. It was an opportunistic business run by a founder who was a true entrepreneur. We never worried about whether we were in stock on anything except shoes, where you have to keep up with a lot of sizes. We were simply trying to empty the warehouse of what my dad had overbought and spread it among the stores, which had to be happy with what they got. "It's like Christmas" was how my dad looked at it. "You don't know what you are getting until you open the package. Now sell it."

In one sense, it was working. It may not have made us recession proof, but the downturn of 1973–75, kicked off in part by the quadrupling of oil prices, had proven we were at least recession resistant. Tough times made people more cost-conscious, and they found their way to us. The recession meant that manufacturers had merchandise piling up because fewer people were buying. We'd buy it at bargain prices. We'd pay $1.10 apiece for 60,000 irregular shirts that others were selling for $10 to $13, and sell them at $5 or two for $7. We'd buy gray velour sport jackets for $7.35 and sell them for $20 as compared to their $60 selling price in department stores, with the manufacturer asking only that we not advertise them by brand name. We were still getting irregulars from Blue Bell, and from many other quality manufacturers of blouses, sweatshirts, and infant wear, and we were buying lots of closeouts.

All in all, it was a unique niche, and it helped explain why Wall

Street had a hard time classifying us. Now that model was facing real pushback. Our own people were telling us that the stuff we were buying and pushing out to the stores wasn't always stuff for which our customers were hungry. We could be doing much better.

We took a look at it strictly from our customers' point of view. They were the same as they'd been since the beginning—they didn't have much money and they needed a retailer who could help them make what they did have go further. To make our approach truly customer driven, we were going to have to do that not just with great buys, but also with the things they needed day to day.

We would call those things "core" items and keep them in stock at all times. It was really that simple, as the best ideas often are. It's amazing in one sense that it didn't occur to us until 1979. Nevertheless, it was an insight that gave us the single greatest growth opportunity we'd ever had. It would drive the company's success for a quarter-century and create a dynamic growth sector for retailing.

The process of strategic planning led us to undertake a 180-degree change in our business model over the course of several years, as we went from a Turner buyer push to our struggling customers' pull upon us. Our system had been overturned completely. As desirable as I thought that was, it was scary for my dad and for me.

The trick was that this new model was going to require us to develop strengths we had never even aspired to have. At the time, Cal Sr. bought—if the price was right, he bought all they had—and had it shipped to the warehouse. Distribution amounted to applying a "warehouse enema" that unloaded whatever he'd bought into the stores. We'd ship them more than they wanted of whatever it was because we needed them to take it off our hands. When that wasn't enough, we had to open more stores because we always had too much inventory and we needed more places to sell it!

Now we were going to keep stores filled with things customers actually needed and wanted. But to stay in stock on an item, you have to keep track of how many you're selling and how many you have. You have to know which stores need which merchandise. That means technology. It calls for logistics and distribution expertise. We had none of that. We had to figure out a road map for change, and decide who in our management team was going to do what. We knew that the tasks that lay before us were enormous.

For all the training we'd received and for all the enthusiasm we brought to the task, we didn't have the wherewithal to undertake strategic planning the AMA way, but that was actually a good thing. If we'd gone into it with all the structure and sophistication they recommended, we would not have been nearly as successful as we were—we'd have been overwhelmed by detail and buried under reports. I think that's what my dad meant by "*plan doing* and not *plan planning.*" His approach was to take the action and observe what worked, giving yourself some latitude to make mistakes along the way. That is creative learning, which, undertaken in response to mistakes, is a very powerful tool. It's something that would serve us well as we moved from my father's autocratic style to the more broadly based planning in which everyone had a stake. It was our way of Dollar Generalizing strategic planning, letting it resonate with our people and our culture.

I came into an entrepreneurial, objective-driven organization, one built on measurable short-term performance targets: "How much are we selling per store?" I spent from 1977 to 1988 trying to transform it into a mission-driven entity: "What is our purpose here?" It's more about knowing that, say, at bottom you are providing low-cost basics to struggling people. Management by objectives, although important, was not my first priority. Results would come as the result of a unifying vision with a clear long-term goal. An organization can get stymied if it operates on nothing more than commands barked from the top. I was interested in the people side of getting things done. I wanted heart, not just brain. Brain can set objectives, and yet performance just might be limited to those objectives. Heart can empower.

My first teacher was my dad, who didn't actually manage with the concept of mission, but who carried it deep inside himself, although he couldn't verbalize or teach it. My job was to take what was inside him and make it work for us as we expanded. Application would be the key. A preacher may discuss the purpose-driven life, but the concept has to be applied one day at a time to one person at a time in his or her specific situation. To do that, you develop processes that work to some degree and then you keep tweaking them. Done well, it can become the underpinning of good leadership.

My take on leadership played out in real time in the stores, as did my dad's, and it was interesting to see the way they intersected. I remember visiting a store once with Margaret and our teenage son. Cal remained standing near the front as Margaret and I walked toward the back, and he overheard one employee say to another, "Do you know who that is?"

Apparently the other didn't, because the first said, "That's Mr. Turner."

The other employee cringed, and the first said, "Don't worry. This isn't the bad one."

My dad was tough. He was the boss. I'd try to be a nice guy, emphasizing teamwork and camaraderie. When my son told me what he'd overheard, I felt bad about this evidence of the downside of my dad's leadership style and thought, *Perhaps my leadership style is more effective.* That lasted until a visit to another store, where I met one of its employees for the first time.

"Mr. Turner," she said, "I'm so pleased to meet you at last. I was told what it would be like."

"What were you told?" I asked her.

"I was told that you would only say good things. You'd be a nice person, very likable, and we'd have a good visit while you were here. Then we would only know what you really thought the next day when the district manager came in and the shit hit the fan!"

My dad's style was to lower the boom on the spot.

"Sam," he would say, "why are those towels displayed like that?"

"Well, Mr. Turner, they say do it that way."

That would get all over my dad.

"Time out, Sam," he would say, his voice booming. "You are now talking to 'they.' Now, let *me* tell you what *they* say. *They* say display the towels *this* way," and he would reposition them the way he thought best.

He went in with answers, with directives and his checklist of things to be done, and when they'd been done wrong, he said something. He always saw things from the customers' perspective. He wanted men's pajamas up on easily reachable shelves where older customers could get at them. When a man goes to the hospital, he reasoned, his wife is going to buy him some pajamas, and if he's an older man, she'll also be older and she shouldn't have to stoop too low to reach them. He wanted our piece goods—our sewing materials—up high as well, as he considered it more likely to be older women who were still sewing.

I would go in with questions. "What's selling?" "What's not?" "How is our work going?" "How can we make it simpler and easier for everyone to serve our customers well?" I was like that throughout my years with the company. I always felt that I was learning. My job in visiting the stores was to create a culture that allowed me to get at the real truth and leave people feeling good about our company. Then I needed to position the right person to act on any problems. In part, it was a demonstration of leadership from ignorance, since I didn't know *how* to straighten out a store!

That Cal Jr. seems like a nice guy, they would think when I'd left. *I wonder what he's really like.* They may have thought I was a closet SOB. With my dad, they knew exactly where they stood in real time.

My approach, though, I considered to be better for our larger company because it stuck with the chain of command. A CEO should not come in and straighten out a store. My dad could create problems for the company because the store manager would say to the district manager, "Mr. Turner said to do it this way." When that happens, the district manager has been blindsided. He can't say, "No, don't pay attention to him." It is the district manager's job to raise Cain if things are wrong, not the CEO's.

I often wondered if the people in the store really got it after my dad left. What they got from him wasn't even principles. It was rules. I'd often stop in stores later and see where they'd taken one of those rules too far, and I could see that if they'd simply put a bit of their own common sense into it, they would have thought, *Yeah, that's what he said, but there's no sense taking it to an extreme.* They didn't get that far in part because our leadership was still in the form of bossism. There were laws, there was a lawgiver, and the most important thing was not to make him angry, so you did what he said, even if doing so created its own problems.

My dad's main concern and mine were the same—to see that our stores were serving our customers well. I just wanted to make sure I was there to support the store and area managers, not confuse them or interfere with their work. I went in with the interpersonal style of my mother, who believed you caught more flies with honey than with vinegar. I wanted to listen to their opinions and motivate them to be creative in solving problems. It was the opposite of the heavy-handed approach of old-school retail operators. I really believe that underneath it all, my father fundamentally agreed with my approach, but was too impatient to use it when he spotted something that needed a quick fix—which was always.

The truth is that our company needed a bit of both management styles. Sometimes problems require a "hit the mule hard on the head" style of management, although that situation usually arose because the Laura Katherine Turner "honey over vinegar" management style hadn't been employed soon enough.

Ultimately we needed employees invested in the betterment of the store, in its mission and its smooth operation. We needed people who cared enough about Dollar General to bring their best thought, their best common sense, to the task. You want them to be thoughtful enough and empowered enough that the shelves are stocked correctly before you get there. You need a good merchandising plan that gets your employees thinking about your customers, and you need clear instructions and clear standards. You want to involve everybody in *How can we do it better?* rather than involving one employee at a time in *How can we fix this mess?*

On the surface, what we did as a company remained the same throughout that twenty-year period. We operated retail stores selling merchandise at low prices, which meant we had to control overhead, coordinate shipping, and do all the other things that go with the retail business. But we had to talk about how those elements could come together in a way that had the inspiration of mission. Doing that would take the company to another level.

We had to transform Dollar General. Fortunately, the same thing that gave us the ability to revolutionize our approach, strategic planning, would give us the day-to-day tools to carry it out. My dad had come to realize that his management style alone was no longer right for our future, and he and I agreed that we would go forward with strategic planning to develop both the company and its leaders. We would bring good people in, develop them to their full potential, and get where we were going together. It was my job to lead the necessary transition.

After we'd refined our definition of core merchandise, we worked to establish the disciplines necessary to stay in stock on those items while still looking for opportunistic buys. We were schizophrenic in a way, with two separate business approaches. Yes, we were focused on basic goods—apparel, shoes, and health and beauty aids—but we were also courting serendipity, scouring the marketplace for bargains we could push through to customers. The former was the new path I wanted us to continue to blaze. The latter was the update of my dad's entrepreneurial opportunism, which was still a big part of the business. Both were part of who we were well into the eighties.

In either case, we had learned that price trumped everything. Once a certain quality threshold was passed, our customers would always buy the cheaper of two items, even if the higher-priced item did offer some incrementally higher quality. We reasoned that if we offered low-price basics every day, our customers would do our advertising by word of mouth. After all, we were in small communities and neighborhoods; word would get around. It wasn't going to take merchandising genius, just the fundamentals of common sense.

Our projections about growth in same-store and new-store sales usually came pretty close, and that surprised us since we still weren't good at connecting all the dots. We knew the strategic planning formula, working from values through mission to strategy to objectives, but in reality we moved from mission statement directly to store and warehouse metrics. We were essentially saying, "This is what we want to be in our stores. How many are we going to open this year?"

Somehow, it worked at first. We didn't have the measurables—heck, we still didn't have a budget—but we had the performance. That was because the concept was sound. Core merchandise and low prices drew in any number of first-time shoppers who then kept coming back. We had three distinct advantages—we had an ever-growing number of stores, so we could draw people who wanted to shop close to home; we were in small towns, so lease rates were low and competition from malls was at a minimum; and we were largely in the South, which was drawing more and more industries from the

Rust Belt, thanks to milder climate, lower wages, "right to work" laws, and a growing labor pool fueled in part by southward migration.

This was true even though the economy was terrible. The last years of the Carter presidency and the beginning of Ronald Reagan's first term were troubled times, with high inflation and a rough business climate. We kept growing anyway. In fact, we had the wind at our back for four or five years. We returned to our classic growth strategy, expanding by increasing same-store sales, by opening individual new stores, and by purchasing the occasional small chain of stores. The UDS and Rankin deals had gone well, but they proved to us that absorbing a major acquisition was extremely challenging.

That kind of quick expansion by acquisition wasn't our style. Besides, we had plenty of growth opportunity left in the markets we already served. We were obviously in a great position.

Meanwhile, we kept growing, sticking to the old pattern of expansion we'd used before the UDS and Rankin acquisitions, but with strategic planning guiding us. We studied things like traffic flow, but we knew that getting too scientific was no guarantee we would discern our best opportunities when it came to picking locations for new stores. It helped that our main warehouse was in Scottsville, twenty miles from Interstate 65 and a one-day drive from much of the country's population. Then it was a matter of finding potential customers with enough income to shop with us regularly. Sometimes it would be a spot where there were already several stores and a lot of traffic, and we'd come in and take our share. Sometimes it was in spots where an existing population was underserved, and we'd fill a void.

We were looking to step up every aspect of the business, and one opportunity came with the retirement of a venerable employee. Years after we'd gone public, we still didn't have consolidated financials or a budget. What we had was a former teacher of high school commercial subjects—bookkeeping, typing, and so forth—named Hubert Craddock, who was in charge of all our bookkeepers.

I walked into my dad's office one day and saw that he was wearing an expression I can only describe as glum.

"What's the matter, Daddy?" I said.

"Hubert has decided to retire early." He was really dejected. Hubert had made stellar contributions to the company and held the title secretary-treasurer. He had common sense and he worked hard and exceeded any reasonable expectation of performance we might have had.

My dad looked up at me. "You've had several accounting courses, so we don't have to replace him, do we?"

"Of course we do," I said.

"Not with somebody expensive," he said, and I knew he meant someone whose salary would be north of $10,000 a year.

"Yes, Daddy, with somebody expensive."

We greeted Hubert's retirement with polar opposite reactions. I was delighted the company could finally position the needed financial oversight by expanding the job's role from accountant to full financial executive, someone who could use the accumulated information for planning and decision making. Dad was dejected, dreading the extra overhead.

We brought in several experienced executives to bolster the company's leadership team. We hired Ed Burke, who had been with the Louisville office of Coopers & Lybrand, as vice president of finance. He would be our first true chief financial officer. We added Bob Carpenter of First American Corporation—I knew him from being on First American's board—as general counsel and vice president of administration. At the same time, we promoted my brother, Steve, to executive vice president of merchandising. There was a good deal of irony in the fact that at the first Hamilton planning meeting, we had listed continuity of management as one of our strengths, yet every time we went back to do more planning, we had just a few of the same executives. Most of the group would be newcomers!

In 1983, as we were firming up that new management team, a St. Louis–based manufacturing and retailing conglomerate named Interco offered to sell us its P. N. Hirsch chain, which consisted of 280 stores in eleven Midwestern and Southern states. Our strategy did not include deals of that magnitude—they had sales of $135 million—but we believed in breaking the rules for the right reasons, and this seemed to be one of those times. We could increase the number of Dollar General stores by 30 percent and our total selling space by 50 percent, something it would otherwise take us three years to do. Actually, what we really wanted was Interco's Eagle Family Discount Stores, located throughout Florida, a marketplace where we needed a larger footprint. At the time, though, the Eagle stores weren't for sale.

We analyzed P. N. Hirsch closely, then bought their outlets in November 1983. Our employees worked like crazy for the next eight months to convert them to DG stores. They were under orders to have the old stores closed no longer than 36 hours before they reopened under the Dollar General banner. We were adamant about getting them all open in time for back-to-school sales. During the first half of 1984, we converted 227 stores, and 53 of those, stretching from Michigan to Louisiana, opened on one day, June 21!

We added 100,000 feet of warehouse space in Scottsville and sales did indeed rise—a quarter of our 1984 sales were from converted Hirsch stores—but all of that was a real hardship for our employees and a strain on the company overall. The level of difficulty that arose in trying to absorb those stores pointed to deeper and broader systemic problems.

I knew for certain those problems weren't because of competition. We had our own niche, operating in markets other retailers didn't want, occupying buildings they bypassed, buying merchandise they ignored, and serving customers they overlooked. No, our troubles were of our own making. We weren't able to match the level of employee training and development Hirsch had been delivering so well. We weren't bringing new employees up to speed fast enough, so there were problems with everything from customer service to record keeping, and our leadership in the field was lacking; we weren't marketing well enough in the new areas, letting potential customers know who we were and what we did. What's more, problems in these new areas distracted us from our core responsibilities. Still, I was hopeful that with the right attitude and the right help, we could recognize and correct our mistakes while maintaining one of our key strengths—our unique ability to retain a sense of perspective, even to laugh at ourselves, and to tap the latent problem-solving genius of our employees.

As the months turned into a year and we still hadn't digested the Hirsch stores, I got nervous—very nervous. As big as the Hirsch acquisition was, I knew if the Eagle deal came through, it would be much bigger and much tougher. The Hirsch stores were in the heartland of our operation and their merchandising and culture were compatible with ours. Converting them was a lot of work, but there was a great deal of common ground. The Eagle stores were in Florida, which was outside our normal operating area, and the company had a culture much different from ours.

We knew the Hirsch stores needed our attention. We needed to settle down, sell some merchandise, and let growth take care of itself. In fact, we said as much to our stockholders. We went on record with them as opposing another acquisition, stressing in our annual report that year that our primary strategy was to build sales in existing stores, with a secondary strategy of increasing the number of stores in operation "in an orderly and profitable manner."

I concentrated on the management areas uniquely my responsibility—planning and people. I was responsible for determining the direction of the company, articulating it to our constituents, and preserving the culture. As we expanded and I was forced to delegate more, I held on to the people-intensive activities—

communicating and the total human development needs of the company. I was also very aware that my name was Turner and that I needed to be a presence in the warehouse and stores. No one wants to work for a bureaucracy.

Then, in February 1984, the CEO of Interco called and told me they were ready to sell the Eagle chain. They were asking $50 million for more than 200 leased stores in prime locations all over Florida, plus a warehouse near Miami. All at once, the possibility was a reality.

We knew it was time to bring on still more help. We added Jim Barton from Ben Franklin Stores as vice president of retail operations and brought two outside directors onto our board—I was now taking their qualifications and their guidance very seriously as we sought the best company performance and direction. One was Herb Wardlow, the former president and COO of Kmart. The other was one of the most important persons in my business life—Larry Appley, the former chairman of the American Management Association.

Shortly after the Hirsch acquisition, I saw that Larry was teaching a management workshop called "Communicating for Productivity" in Santa Barbara. I was surprised he was still alive, much less active, since I knew he had to be eighty. I had been extremely impressed by him when I took his "Management Course for Presidents" more than fifteen years earlier, and the two courses I'd taken in 1978 helped us implement strategic planning and kick off five years of amazing growth. I wasn't going to pass up the chance to learn more about communication from the quintessential communicator.

Larry was a true legend. He had developed the AMA's strategic planning model. He had been on dozens of boards and had won the Presidential Medal of Merit for his work for various government agencies before and during World War II. He was the author of several books, including *Management in Action*.

Larry conducted the sessions himself, and he was as impressive as ever. The course dealt with how to communicate as a leader and how to connect with people, and it added a great deal to what I'd learned from him earlier.

Knowing we were about to do the Eagle acquisition, I arranged for a one-on-one meeting. A growth company needs great management, and I knew we needed Larry to help us establish a system that would let us develop it. We sat down and began talking. We had a lot in common. I learned he was a Methodist minister's son and had other ministers and a bishop in his family. We really clicked on a personal level. Finally, I turned to business.

"Larry," I said, "the AMA has its stamp all over my company. We've just gone through the best five years in the company's history, strictly following the AMA's model of strategic planning. Now we're about to undertake an acquisition that scares the bejeebers out of me, and I don't think we have the management development programs in place to prepare us for what's coming. In less than a year and half, we're going to add fifty percent more stores. I'm worried the company could get into trouble. We need the right plan and the right management to carry it out. We need your management development program as a complement to strategic planning, and we need people trained as well as only you can help us train them."

I paused for a moment.

"I want you to be a consultant to our company."

"I don't consult for companies unless I'm on the board," he said.

"Well, then," I said, "I'd like you to come on our board."

"I can't do that. I'm fully booked this year and next. I have no place on my calendar."

"Look, Larry," I said. "I don't think you understand what I'm saying. I wasn't asking you. I'm telling you that you don't have a choice. There's so much at stake here. The planning our company has put in place is your doing. Your protégé Hank Pattison taught us what we know. And look at our common roots! We're even fellow Methodists!"

I watched a tear roll down his cheek. Apparently, we had connected. "Well," he said, "I'll see what I can do."

I went home, knowing I had to get my dad to buy into the plan. I told him about Larry and said I wanted him on the board. I'm not sure he was sold on the idea, but he said, "All right. If he's eighty, he won't be around too long anyway!" My dad was a dozen years younger.

Larry resigned from the boards of two other companies and joined Dollar General. We agreed that he would give us three days a month to help us get the management development program in place.

Larry turned out to be as much soul mate as mentor to me. He had never had a son, and he kind of looked at me in that way. My dad had been and always would be my mentor, and only he could ever be a true father figure in my life, but Larry gave me something beyond what my father could give, something vital as I tried to move the company forward. At that point in my career, I needed both of them desperately.

12

A Company Out of Control

The relationship between Larry Appley and my dad started off cordially enough, but that didn't last long. Larry was going to help us move from family business to professionally run company. My dad *embodied* the family business. He felt about strategic planning the way he felt about computers. If it said we should do something he agreed with, it was superfluous. If it said something he disagreed with, it would just anger him. Until the end of his life, Larry's perspective brought out the very worst in my dad, who hated what happened to the company from the moment Larry joined. Given the radical difference in their approaches, it makes sense in hindsight. I remember Larry saying to me, "You need to sound more professional as the CEO of a large company. When you reference your father, don't call him Daddy."

"But that's who he is!" I said.

Meanwhile, we were still wrestling with the Eagle proposal. I knew why we shouldn't do it. Most of their stores were in large cities. Most of ours were in small towns. Our headquarters, our ethos, and our entire identity were firmly ensconced in Scottsville. They catered to a male customer. We catered to a female customer. While DG sold clothing and basic consumables, Eagle sold sporting, automotive, electrical, and plumbing goods, along with swimming pool chemicals and accessories. To top it off, more than 40 percent of their sales were cigarettes, which we didn't sell and didn't want to.

There were still more reasons. Our people had gone through hell with the Hirsch acquisition, and we still hadn't digested those stores. We were understaffed, with ten vacant district manager positions. Our advertising expenses were up and we needed money to build a third warehouse.

In spite of all that, we were torn. Here was the opportunity we had wanted a year earlier, the chance to enter, on a large scale, a ripe and lucrative market. I called a meeting of the planning group, comprised of some of our key executives, and looked for consensus. Ultimately, we were smart enough collectively to know we couldn't do it, and we declined Interco's initial proposal. Then they lowered the price. We looked still more closely and saw that the "goodwill" for which they wanted $10 million was vastly overrated; the price came down some more. The cost per square foot of some of Florida's most promising retail locations kept getting lower. I knew that we'd never have an opportunity like this for positioning ourselves in one of the country's fastest-growing states. I have to admit that I was starry-eyed. So was my dad and everyone in senior management, and that's a dangerous thing.

Finally we all decided the deal was too good to pass up. We bought the stores in February 1985 for $35 million. We had our entrée into Florida. As he had with Hirsch, Steve would direct the transition. We gave ourselves six months to convert 206 stores. We would liquidate the merchandise that didn't fit our customers and reopen Eagle outlets as Dollar General stores. I was weary, but I jumped for joy when my dad said, "Son, you and the management team have done a wonderful thing. I'm proud of you and excited about what's ahead for our company."

As we looked at what we had bought, though, we recognized that there were as many problems as possibilities. I went to Florida for a visit. The warehouse complex, in Opa-locka, consisted of several dilapidated World War II–era hangars, and the corporate culture was totally different from ours. Eagle had even fewer systems in place than we did, and management discipline seemed to be lacking. There was also a major communication problem—the company's employees were largely non-English-speaking Cubans.

While I was there, someone mentioned "our vet."

"You mean veterinarian?" I said.

"Yes."

"What does he do for us?"

"He works on the horses."

My goodness, I thought. *What have we really acquired here?*

It took a good deal of back-and-forth for me to figure that one out. We did indeed have a veterinarian in our employ. He couldn't practice his given profession, because he was licensed in Cuba, not the United States. The only employment he could get was an hourly warehouse job with Eagle, and in one of life's great ironies, Eagle had placed him in charge of repairing the coin-operated mechanical horses that sat in front of stores. It certainly made poetic if not logical sense.

Such was the culture of those Eagle stores that this Dollar General CEO spent a good deal of time during that familiarization tour in various states of wonder and consternation, and it wasn't lost on me that we'd have been much better served if I'd visited the warehouse during working hours before our purchase, rather than accepting their offer of a nighttime tour that gave no hint of the chaos I was now seeing. We had worked for months inspecting every store and every store lease, looking at their merchandise, their prices, their store locations, operations, and customers, but we hadn't taken this peek behind the warehouse curtain.

I had taken Steve with me on that trip, and he and I were talking to employees through an interpreter. At one stop, I introduced him.

"This is my brother, Steve," I said. "He will be down here working with you."

The interpreter pointed at Steve, and as he repeated what I'd said in Spanish, Steve and I distinctly heard the word *yeh-ho*. Steve's eyes got huge and no doubt mine did too. He looked at me with a face that said, *Did he just call me a yeh-ho?*

Again, it took some thinking and asking after we'd walked away, but it seems he was using the word *viejo*, which normally means "old." Don't ask me why that word seemed useful to him. It was the example of the imperfect mash-up of redneck and Hispanic we faced as we began trying to blend these cultures. I left hoping that once the company was exposed to the DG mission and spirit from top to bottom, they'd come around.

We began the long, expensive, and exhausting process of converting stores again, closing the Eagle office and running the operation out of Scottsville. We had managers in other stores who hadn't seen their district managers in months because the DMs had been off helping open stores. Our warehouses and trucking operations and our office and merchandising staffs were all overloaded. Our 1985 sales increased by $100 million to $584 million, with four-fifths of that increase in Florida, but our expenses rose even more on a percentage basis, and we experienced a 13 percent drop in income. The cost of operating a Hirsch or Eagle store was much higher than that of running a Dollar General store, and shrinkage, the difference between inventory in the accounting records and inventory on hand, was unacceptably high. We hoped that was simply an outgrowth of the process of converting stores and not the other possibility—theft.

Over the next year, the situation got worse. Serving Florida stores from warehouses in Scottsville and Dumas, Arkansas, was costly and disruptive, further increasing employee turnover, which was already too high among Eagle-turned-DG employees. When shrinkage stayed high and seemed to spread to older Dollar General stores, we hired someone with a background in internal security and management information systems and created a position for him that included both.

We had been stretched to our limit as a company by the acquisitions. We had grown by 50 percent and we weren't handling the growth well. Earnings plummeted. Gary Dennis, an analyst at J. C. Bradford & Co., said the business had outgrown family management. The company was woefully behind in terms of systems and infrastructure. The press noticed. *The New York Times* said a weak management team had bungled our rapid expansion. Since I was someone for whom life and business were pretty much the same thing, it was hard for me not to take it personally. I could lose sleep in good times over what we might be missing. It was worse during this period, although I did find that reading theology at bedtime helped with the insomnia!

The one bright spot was that at least one analyst knew we had been doing something right because of our long history of growth and liked our potential to turn our present troubles around in a year or two. In the meantime, it wasn't just the rapid growth giving us problems. We weren't executing well on the basics. We had always operated with a small upper-level staff and we needed systems that could handle this new and larger organization. We had to undertake what I called at the time "a serious re-examination of all major business assumptions and practices of the company." We asked the tough questions about why earnings had gone to pot and what had gone wrong with the new stores. We saw that in addition to weaknesses in management, we weren't doing a good job of merchandising our company in markets different from those in our Kentucky and Tennessee base.

In the fall of 1986, I restructured the company. I brought in a new vice president of marketing who would also oversee advertising. Steve would oversee buying, store operations, and distribution. Ed Burke would remain at the head of finance, our new security chief would oversee data processing, and Bob Carpenter would run human resources.

We brought all the senior executives together in Hamilton to chart a course. We poured ourselves again into strategic planning. As Larry looked over the company, his eye lit on our mission statement: "To serve better than anyone else does our customer's need for quality basic merchandise at everyday low prices." He had real problems with that, recognizing it as the long, unwieldy, and off-base statement it was. He said, "It's not a mission statement when you compare yourself to the competition. A mission statement is about you, your unique situation, and the opportunities you want to strive for."

We began as a group to come up with a new one, and eventually we hit on one as short and simple as it was lofty—"Serving Others," which held echoes for me of the gospel song "Others," which Miss Havelon had sung so beautifully at Camp Dunroamin when I was a boy. It was a great example of someone who had an impact far beyond what she would ever know—in this case, on a Fortune 500 company.

We re-examined our business strategy, assigning each executive the task of developing an operating plan to achieve his or her department's goals. We were going to share those plans in December.

I wasn't immune to learning from these sessions either. One in particular reminded me of Luther Turner's default position, that there is something to learn from everyone, no matter which side of the classroom or leadership aisle you're on. I was speaking to senior executives at a leadership development training program, telling them about the importance of a personal mission statement. I told them the elements—that a mission should be brief and motivating, something you could never fully accomplish but which would help you screw your head on straight every day. I shared Dollar General's mission statement—"Serving Others"—and then, as I encouraged them to write their personal mission statements down, I shared mine. At the time, mine was, "Rejoicing in my God-given potential and developing it to the fullest in a way that encourages others to do the same." It was actually quite a mouthful, given what I had just said about brevity, and when I'd finished, a shy, bespectacled man named Allen Bullard came up to me and said, "Mr. Turner, I want to share my mission statement with you. I think it meets your test. It really helps me every day to get *my* head screwed on right and to motivate me, and it's only three words—"God-honoring change."

I thought, *Wow! That's what mine is trying to say!* Here I was telling them how to do it, and I didn't have it nailed down nearly as well as he did. He had captured the essence of my mission statement in a distinct and memorable way. He said, "In every unique circumstance, with whatever persons are involved, I think, 'My mission here is the change that honors God,' and that's what I'm motivated to do." It was one of those cases when the trainee had gotten it more right than the trainer. I presented "okay," and he had returned "great." I chose to follow his lead. "God-honoring change" has been my personal mission statement ever since.

All the sessions seemed to be going well, but then in December, when the senior executives met to go over our progress on operating plans, no one had held planning sessions and there were no plans. Everything was still unraveling. We had little presence in the stores, an eroding customer base in many areas, and no real system to provide unity. "It was a matter," said one of our executives, "of trying to hold the thing together with chewing gum and paper clips."

Then came the big blow. Ed Burke, our CFO, walked into my office one morning in the spring and said our auditing firm was suggesting that we not announce our financial results until we checked with our lenders.

"Ed," I said, "we've never believed in sitting on our financial results. We announce them when we have them."

"But Cal," he said, "we have covenant violations in our term loan agreement, and if we don't get a waiver, our lenders could use them as a basis for calling it in. And we can't cover the loan. We could be forced into Chapter 11."

I was devastated. Our chief financial officer was suggesting the possibility of bankruptcy. Sales in 1986 had dropped for the first time in the company's history. Net income was down from $17 million to just $4 million. Shrinkage alone dwarfed that number—$22 million in merchandise had simply disappeared! It was obvious that we were in big trouble.

I had to face the fact that I was not in control of the company. None of us was. We stepped up internal security and hired investigators. We studied the Florida stores, which alone had one-third of the shrinkage, and found undertrained, undermotivated, sometimes resentful employees, and the picture didn't improve as you went up the chain of command. We uncovered theft at every level of the organization, from store clerks to the area manager and some of our buyers. We fired 400 people and 150 of them were arrested. Turnover among managers and clerks hit 200 percent, meaning on average, every position was turning over twice a year. Our bookkeepers were overwhelmed, and as much as it pained me, I knew our CFO was not up to the job in a company this size; he had to be replaced.

We had been like a teenager whose jeans are too short because he is growing so rapidly. He will get used to that, since it's pretty normal, but if he really has a spurt of growth, he'll burst the rear end right out of them, and that is what happened to us. Our butt was showing.

All of this might have been much easier if our family had been pulling in one direction, but it wasn't. While in many ways we still thought of the company as a family business, it had to be operated as a true public company. The stresses of our rapid growth meant we had to resolve some fundamental family issues. We needed a unified vision and that didn't exist. Steve and I were apples and oranges—or more exactly, I was a Turner and he was a Goad, my mother's side of the family. He studied philosophy. I studied business administration. He was a thoughtful debater. I was a decision maker who was now forced to make those decisions in haste.

Plain old sibling rivalry was part of the deal. It wasn't my fault. It wasn't his. We just viewed the world differently, and had different visions for the company that couldn't be reconciled. I love him deeply and he loves me, yet we were not effectively working together.

As CEO, I was responsible for the entire company, concentrating on human resources, planning, and administration. Steve was responsible for merchandising, distribution, and store operations. Neither of us was thrilled with the job the other was doing. I thought that we were losing our edge in opportunistic buying and that indecisive merchandising leadership was hurting us. I had to fire the general merchandising manager, who reported to Steve, and I became convinced that we had become a "buying" rather than a "selling" culture and that some sort of fundamental shift had to take place.

Part of Steve's restlessness had to do with Scottsville.

"You have your Nashville friendships and business connections," he said. "I'm not intellectually stimulated by talking to a cow in the field."

Steve had been lobbying for some time for us to move the company headquarters from Scottsville to Nashville, motivated primarily, I thought, by a desire to move to Nashville himself. I resisted.

"Steve," I said, "Scottsville is central to the culture of our company. It's where it was founded. Our roots are here. Let's get back to the important issues we're working on. Let's not let ourselves be distracted by this discussion."

I finally convinced him to let it go for a time, but it came up again in strategic planning. We discussed whether we had outgrown Scottsville as a corporate home. Some people just aren't cut out to live in small towns, and we knew that was a factor in limiting the kind of first-rate people we needed to attract to senior management. Nashville, because of its size, industries, universities, and culture, had much more to offer potential hires. Steve was right. Moving was something we were going to have to do.

That left my dad. No matter whose idea this was, I was going to have to broach the subject with him and then do the negotiating. It was not going to be easy.

"Son," he told me with fire in his eyes, "I admit I'm emotional about this, but I know I'm right. This company needs to stay here. Sam Walton stayed in Bentonville and that company's done pretty well!"

My dad went so far as to buy a company helicopter to go with the company plane we'd picked up in the UDS acquisition. He figured we could use it to fly to stores, and he thought if his boys could use it for quick hops to Nashville, they might be persuaded to forget this move. It didn't work, and it turned out to be a bad investment as well as a source of embarrassment for Howard Johnson, who handled store leasing.

"I hated to fly to some little town in a helicopter," he said, "and talk to a guy about a dollar and a half a square foot when my trip there cost six hundred dollars."

My dad asked me to talk to John Holland, who had moved the Fruit of the Loom headquarters from New York to Bowling Green, so I went to visit him. I told him about the discussion and he said, "Well, Cal, I think moving to Nashville would be the smartest thing you could do." I never did tell my dad what John had said because I saw in John someone who could be a great asset for our board, and I didn't want my dad angry at him.

166 • MY FATHER'S BUSINESS

I was ready for us to make the decision, but when I checked the company bylaws, I discovered that the location of the corporate office was a board decision, not a management decision. I knew that wouldn't work because the board was aligned with my dad. The only votes we had were mine, Steve's, and Larry Appley's.

Fortunately, I also knew that nobody really knew or paid attention to the bylaws, so I went into the next board meeting and said, "I'm announcing management's decision to locate the corporate office in Nashville."

Well, that meeting got hot. The *only* person to side with me was Larry Appley. Ed Burke said nothing. *Steve* said nothing. My dad got so emotional he left the room.

When the meeting finally ended, Steve asked to meet privately. We went into my office and closed the door.

"Cal Jr.," he said, "there was a lot of emotion in that meeting."

"You're telling me!" I said.

"Well, I think we need to pay attention to emotion. Do you think we really ought to do this?"

I said, "Steve! Are you saying that you've changed your mind? Are you saying moving to Nashville isn't the right thing for us to do?"

"No," he said, "but there was a lot of emotion there."

"Look," I told him. "The last thing the Turner boys need to do is to throw in the towel on this. We've taken a stand and it's the right thing to do. We need to proceed."

And that's what we did. We opened an 8,000-square-foot executive office in Green Hills, an upscale section of Nashville, and moved a dozen top executives there late in 1986 in what amounted to a headquarters for our strategic planning division. That would fit nicely with the management resources development program we had initiated. We also transferred more than 100 persons in our accounting, human resources, insurance, and security departments to a 25,000-square-foot building we bought and renovated in downtown Scottsville, where we still had a huge presence. We had more than 500 office employees with a payroll of more than $8 million and our largest warehouse there. We paid $133,000 in county and city property taxes and $88,000 in city payroll taxes.

But Nashville would now be headquarters. Ironically, it wouldn't be long after the move that Steve's tenure with the company would end. We'd be selling the helicopter too.

13

✿

The Toughest Decision of My Life

Our new presence in Nashville made it easier to draw high-level executive talent, and also made it easier for us to lead without Cal Sr. interference, although he was still looking over our shoulders from Scottsville. All of us did have the opportunity to mature in decision making.

Early in 1987, we reorganized the company, dividing it into three broad areas—operations, finance, and development. We brought in some of the best business minds we could find, including a high-powered executive, Bruce Quinnell, as our CFO, in order to establish greater financial control as we dealt particularly with shrinkage. He would also have primary responsibility for investor relations, so it wouldn't take so much of my time. We hired a new executive vice president to lead the company's strategic planning effort, also giving him responsibilities in marketing, MIS, and human resources. I wanted to see if he could be groomed as a future CEO. We added John Holland of Fruit of the Loom and Jim Cockman, a senior executive with Sara Lee, as directors. Within that group, Dollar General had the workings of a great and, for the first time in the twenty years we'd been a public company, truly independent board.

A new SEC requirement of us as a public company was that our board have an audit committee comprised of qualified, independent directors. I decided to ask Wallace Rasmussen, the crusty former CEO of Beatrice Foods, whom I had met on the board of Shoney's, to join our board and chair the audit committee.

Wallace had worked his way up from a job as an ice hauler to president and CEO of Beatrice, earning a reputation along the way for what *The Wall Street Journal* called a "pugnacious style" that "made enemies." He was a savvy operator who understood hardball. He'd forced the resignation of his designated successor, Beatrice chairman William G. Mitchell. I knew that if you had a fight coming, you wanted him on your side. The situation with Steve was tense, and in the back of my mind I knew it might come to a head one day. I wanted to lay out the situation before bringing Wallace on board.

"You need to know something," I told him, "in case it would change your mind about coming on our board. I may have to fire my brother."

"No, that's okay," he said. "But when do we handle the old man?"

I was shocked.

"Wallace," I said, "he's not a problem."

"Okay," he said. "We shall see. We shall see."

Once everyone was in place, we put together new management and merchandising teams and adopted an operations initiative. With outside consultants, we examined distribution, which we decided to consolidate and automate, and we made our first major investment in technology to get us into a database environment.

Overexpansion had led us to the most intensive implementation of strategic planning in DG's history. Now, our new management team was conducting a serious re-examination of all the major business assumptions and practices of the company. Bruce was appalled to find out that we didn't pay store employees with checks. The store manager paid them out of the cash drawer, filled out vouchers, and mailed them to Scottsville. That was the extent of the paper trail! Bruce was adamant that we needed more control over the millions of dollars that went out to thousands of employees across the country.

My dad had taken the common-sense position that we didn't really have control of the cash in the stores anyway and that this saved a step and a great deal of manpower and paperwork. We handled the IRS forms and payments from Scottsville, and the system had worked since the beginning.

It was time for yet another aspect of the company to enter the present age, though, and Bruce came up with a payroll system to accomplish that. It drove everybody nuts for a while, but eventually it got smoothed out and employees got their checks out of Scottsville.

Amid this flurry of activity, it was obvious within a matter of weeks that our new executive vice president wasn't a good fit for the company—he and Steve just didn't get along, among other things—and we let him go. It was also apparent that Steve and I had work to do. The Turners were going to have to get control of the company.

"Steve," I said, "I've studied the fourteen acquisitions our company has done to date. I've been involved in all of them, and the common denominator for all of those troubled companies was a problem at the top. If the Turners don't get their act together, we're going to face the same situation. Merchandising and operations are both broken."

Merchandising—turning cash into merchandise your customers want, then turning that merchandise back into more cash—is the fundamental dynamic of any retail company, and it was also the prime mover of our family dilemma.

"Merchandising is okay," Steve said. "It's not going to change. You take operations and run it the way you want." I wanted our new people running both. I offered Steve the chance to head the real estate development of the company. He knew that would remove him from the day-to-day mainstream and he wanted nothing to do with it.

"If I can't be actively involved in running the business," he said, "I'm not going to do it."

"Then *act* like a chief operating officer!" I told him. "Let's agree on an agenda for the development of the company. Bring me your budget for the next year."

Steve got together with his own group of executives and came back with an action plan that was long on plan and short on action. It didn't impress me at all. It felt as if my brother and I were at a complete impasse.

No amount of creativity or strategic planning could succeed in the face of this split between the Turner brothers. There was a Cal camp and a Steve camp. With my dad in the picture, it amounted to a full three-ring circus at the top! The vision needed at our company simply did not exist. Something had to change, and it was up to me to change it. After all, I had been the family's Mr. Fix-It since I was a boy and had to tell my grandfather he couldn't drive anymore. I stewed for a while, then went to Scottsville in the spring of 1987 to visit my father.

"Daddy," I said, "I'm forty-seven years old and I'm making an *adult decision*. I can't stay in business with my brother."

"Steve can't run the company!" he said.

I'm not sure I can run the company either! I thought. But then, I didn't know who could.

"This just isn't working for me," I said. "You and Steve and I need to talk about what that means. I'm willing to accept responsibility for my decision and leave the company if it comes to that."

We tried for several months to work through it as a family. Steve, my dad, my mother, and my sisters just hoped I'd get over it somehow. Our sister Laura Jo was angry at Steve and angrier at me as all this was going on.

"Cal Jr.," she said, "you and Steve are brothers. Why can't the two of you go into a room, shut the door, and work this out?"

I thought for a while. Knowing she and Betty had troubles of their own, I said, "Laura Jo, let me ask you this. Could you do that with our sister?"

"Heck no!" she said.

I didn't want to fire Steve, but something had to give.

He and I talked, and he told me that under no circumstances would he resign. "This company is family," he said, "and I couldn't resign from it any more than I could resign from the family. If I ever leave, you'll have to fire me."

We were different in that way. Yes, it was family for me, too, but it was my job to take the company beyond that. Steve's comment let me know just what I'd have to do if it came down to it. I understood him well enough to know this came from his heart. He had vested family identity in the company even more than I had. As much as this was my father's business, I believe Steve looked at it as his father's business to an even greater extent. I love that about him, but given the situation, it added an extra burden as I tried to reach a decision.

We brought in a psychologist to help Steve and me communicate. The psychologist would stand behind me and paraphrase what I was really trying to say. Then he'd get behind Steve and paraphrase him. Once, after Steve had finished, the psychologist looked at me and said, "Cal Jr., you are a self-righteous son of a bitch."

Steve jumped and I did too.

"Well, yes, I guess I am," I said. "Somehow in the stress and strain of this relationship, that may be what I've become."

We were in an impossible situation. I talked now and then to trusted confidants, turning especially to friends in the Young Presidents' Organization forum. We could be honest with one another, which was something that usually could not happen elsewhere. It's an occupational hazard of the top of an organization that you're protected from the truth. People have a lot of reasons for not giving it to you straight. In this group, though, we bonded, talking about business and personal matters, and so we had a history. We had each other's permission to say, "You're full of crap," when the occasion warranted.

I was talking with them about what we were going through when one of them turned to me and said, "Cal, I think Dollar General may be a dinosaur, an extinct species still walking around." As dramatic as that statement was, it was in line with what I knew about the fact that we had to change dramatically, although it was obvious we hadn't yet hit on the best kind of change. Another said, "Cal, we've been listening to you talk about the dynamics between you and your brother, and you keep saying, 'I think it's getting better. I think we'll get beyond this stuff.' We've heard that for so long that we all know it's not going to get any better. Your relationship with your brother has a fatal flaw within it—the sibling rivalry the two of you can't get beyond. It's also obvious to us that you're not willing to do anything to change it."

My friends were telling me I was not being a good steward of the company unless I put into motion the change it needed. However daunting that change could be, given my relationship with Steve, they were reminding me that sometimes you either let an impossible situation go on indefinitely or you become an agent of change. My personal mission was God-honoring change and my highest value was reconciling love, which pursues the change that honors God. I had to ask myself how committed I was to both precepts.

I had gone in with one question, which had moved pretty rapidly to another and then to this one, and ironically it was my brother who helped me arrive at the bottom line. As much as I hated to have to be the one to ask whether I should fire my brother, I had to ask it. *I have to be willing*, I thought, *to accept the responsibility of asking the question that can break up our family, but which the business, the public corporation, has a crying need for me to answer as CEO.*

I was not taking full accountability as CEO of the company

because of the constraints I felt having my brother as the number two officer. We wanted to do different things with the company, but I had to remember that I was the one ultimately responsible for it. I was going to have to step up to bat and assume responsibility. Dollar General had three power bases—a father and two sons—and I had let myself feel that I wasn't really responsible because I didn't fully feel like the CEO. I could see that the company, if it had one fully positioned CEO, one goal, one direction, could do well. I was that person on paper, but I now had to *be* and perform as that person.

Following a tough course of action is seldom a straightforward proposition. There are all sorts of twists and turns, layers and motives we can't see going in. It takes courage. It takes openness. It also takes grounding, a rootedness in God, that can give a firm place to stand even when all around is changing.

I was going to have to get my head on straight. In fact, I had really been trying, amid all the turmoil of the last few years, to look for a little more order and balance in my life. My dad always felt that a retailer needed to devote all his time and energy to business, but that wasn't how I looked at it. I liked preaching the occasional sermon at the Scottsville Methodist Church, and I wanted to be active in its music program—a lot of wonderful "little old ladies" wanted me to sing at their funerals. I also wanted to get my golf and tennis games back in shape and occasionally hit the ski slopes with my son.

Everybody needs someplace to go when he doesn't have the answer. Late in 1987, I went skiing. I was trying to get my head clear, but my mind was on the business and the problems with Steve and me. I was hurting, and the pain and stress of the process literally drove me to my knees. I had to go to my God. I wasn't a daily Bible reader, as a good Bible Belt Methodist is supposed to be, but in the face of that crisis, my reading of the scripture became one of crying inquiry. I read intently, and I got the conviction I needed in the fifteenth chapter of John: "I am the true vine, and my Father is the vinedresser. Every branch in me that does not bear fruit, he takes away, and every branch that does bear fruit he prunes, so that it may bear more fruit."

That seemed to be God's marching orders regarding my father's business, and it involved both Turner brothers. Steve would undergo the pain of being taken away from the company. I had to undergo the pain of cutting away any excuses I had for not being able to lead within this family dynamic. Only with that kind of pruning could we as a company bear more fruit.

I had to assume responsibility and take on the full yoke of leadership. We desperately needed clarity in decision making, not two camps jockeying for position. I was responsible for firing Steve. I was responsible for putting everything back together and making it okay. It was the Mr. Fix-It part of my personality on steroids.

Still, it was very difficult for me to go forward with what I knew would be a painful rending of company and family. Making a decision is one thing. Carrying it out can be pure hell. When I got back to the office after my skiing trip and found things somehow better between Steve and me, I began to waver.

I was accustomed to giving advice more than receiving it, but this was such a critically important decision that I knew I needed the perspective of someone I trusted. I spoke at length to the senior pastor at my church, and he didn't try to dissuade me from what I knew I needed to do.

Not long afterward I came across another scripture. It was from 2 Corinthians 3, and it said, "Therefore having such a hope, we act with great boldness." I read it as God telling me, "I've told you what to do; now get your butt in gear."

This was the hardest thing I ever had to do, and it was Steve who forced the issue and actually helped me carry out the decision. We were talking again in January 1988 about a move for him into the real estate side of the business. It was a repeat of the conversation we'd had months earlier. He wanted to stay in merchandising, and he wasn't going to change the way it was operating.

"Steve," I said, "it needs to change."

"It isn't going to change," he said. "Not under me."

"It has to," I said.

"This company is my birthright as much as it is yours," he said. "I'm a Turner too. If you insist on this change, brother, you're going to have to step up to the plate and deny me my birthright. You're going to have to fire me and live with that the rest of your life."

I answered him with the words from the wedding vow. "I do." With that, my brother was fired.

I can't tell you how hard that moment and the next days and weeks were. As it sank in for both of us what had just happened, he said, "The first thing we have to do is call Mama and Daddy in Florida," where they spent January and February every year. We knew they'd be devastated.

"I can't believe, in a company this big, I've raised two sons who can't get along," said our dad. Our mother said, "I love you both, but if I were there, I'd spank you both."

To his credit, my dad called me the next day and said, "Son, I haven't slept at all since that call, but it has come to me that just as an animal cannot survive with two heads, neither can a company. You did what you had to do and you have my full support."

It was a wonderful thing to hear at a time when I was really hurting.

For years afterward, though, my dad would revisit Steve's firing. He may have agreed that it was the right thing to do, but he had a terrible time adjusting to it, and every time he brought it up, it was like a dagger through my heart. I'd have to go back and talk him through it and help him process it again. The last time he brought it up, I said, "Daddy, let me try this on you. How would you like to be in business with Uncle Frank?"

He and Uncle Frank often fought like cats and dogs at Farmers National Bank board meetings. One would say "no" simply because the other had said "yes." He closed his eyes for a moment and I could almost see his reliving those fights. It was the Goad-Turner divide, the same one that ran like a river between Steve and me. My dad and Frank loved each other, just as Steve and I did, but that didn't make it any easier for them to deal with each other. I had finally hit on something that let him understand why it didn't work for Steve and me to be in the same business.

"Ohhh," he said, sighing. "I understand, son. I'm okay with it now."

The next step was to tell the world about Steve's departure. It would have been so wonderful if we could have handled it quietly, but as a public company we didn't have that option. I crafted a press release that painted the best possible face on it.

Steve said, "Well, you can put this nice spin on it all you want, but I'm going to tell all my friends you fired me."

"Steve," I said, "we can't handle it that way."

"Well, you handle it the way you want. You've got the company now, but I'm going to tell my friends that you fired me."

He was right. I had the company, and whatever he did, it was time for me to move it in the right direction.

Then, in July of that year, our mother died after a brief illness. Laura Katherine Turner was the glue that had held us all together, and her death marked a paradigm shift in the family's history. She saw to it that the family gathered to celebrate birthdays and holidays, and she was at the center of every event. In her later years she was a healthy distraction from the business for my father, getting him to Florida for as long as two months in the winter, something all of us needed. She had the prescience, as her health grew worse, to know that my dad would come barreling back into the picture once she was gone, and she knew how that was going to affect me. In fact, the last thing she said to me was, "I'm worried about the load you are going to have to carry."

She had battled cancer four years earlier—the weight she lost allowed her to get into her wedding dress on their fiftieth anniversary. When the pain had returned, all of us went with her to Vanderbilt University Medical Center for tests. The doctor could barely get it out when he told us the cancer was back and that there was nothing anyone could do for her.

Mama's reaction was frustration. She had had a healthy and happy life and was prepared for the end, but she didn't want to go through the pain and suffering that was coming, and even more than that, she didn't want us to have to watch someone we loved die.

"Why don't you just take me out back and shoot me?" she said. It was pain and love speaking, her way of saying that the end couldn't come too soon.

The family gathered around her at the end—she lingered about a month after the diagnosis—and took care of her. It helped to bring us a little closer together at a time when everyone was still upset by Steve's firing a few months earlier.

The entire community of Scottsville grieved with our family, yet another manifestation of the wonderful heritage of small-town life.

An early family photo of Josiephine and Luther Turner with a
dapper young Calister Turner.
(Courtesy of Turner Family)

A peaceful Cal Turner, Sr., in
the yard at home. *(Courtesy of
Turner Family)*

My favorite photo of
Laura Katherine Turner.
(Courtesy of Turner Family)

Probably the last photo of me with a
full head of hair! *(Courtesy of Turner
Family)*

Head table at our store party, with the entire Turner family there. *(Courtesy of Turner Family)*

Proud profile of my dad, driving the 1955 Pontiac of Grandma Turner. *(Courtesy of Turner Family)*

The original warehouse in Scottsville—the big brick building was bought at half price! *(Courtesy of Dollar General)*

Another gangbuster store opening, this one in 1958. *(Courtesy of Dollar General)*

My officer candidate school
photograph, fall 1962.
(Courtesy of Turner Family)

The "highest tech" activity of opening a Dollar General store in the early days. *(Courtesy of Dollar General)*

A wonderful light moment in Cal Sr.'s office. (Excuse my garish tie!) *(Courtesy of Turner Family)*

I don't know which Cal Turner is talking! We are about to board the company helicopter. *(Courtesy of Dollar General)*

Backstage at the Grand Ole Opry: Roy Acuff, Margaret and Cal Turner, and Mr. & Mrs. Ed Moelhing. *(Courtesy of Dollar General)*

Cal Sr. receiving an Honorary Doctorate ("Doctorate of Donations") from Lindsey Wilson College. *(Courtesy of Turner Family)*

A magazine cover in 1987, with a quote that got me in trouble with shareholders. *(Courtesy of Advantage Magazine)*

The great occurrence of 1988: receiving an award for private sector initiatives from Ronald Reagan in a Rose Garden ceremony. *(Courtesy of Dollar General)*

Checking a store display with someone who understands it much better than I do. *(Courtesy of Dollar General)*

A 1998 Christmas photo of three Cal Turners and the brand new Hurley Calister Turner IV. *(Courtesy of Turner Family)*

14

A Family and Company Divided

Not long after Mama died, my dad did turn his attention to the company. In his grief at losing his lifelong sweetheart, the business he had founded became his lifeline. One of the things that caught his attention was a management information systems proposal, which he set about opposing. We were trying to get more of our computing and informational needs met, since we were disastrously behind when it came to technology. Our company was too big not to be more up-to-date, and our new CFO, Bruce Quinnell, had a major proposal to take to the board.

Mentioning computers to my dad was still like waving red in front of a bull.

"Son," he said to me on the Wednesday before a Friday board meeting in November, "if you even take that proposal to the board, I may resign."

I knew I'd better advise the board that this would not be a routine meeting. I called together the local directors and set up a conference call with the rest. I told them what was happening.

Wallace Rasmussen reacted as he had before he had come on the board.

"Cal," he said, "this company is very vulnerable now. You have new management that has come aboard in support of your leadership. We're in a turnaround situation, and we have a fiduciary responsibility to the shareholders to make it work. We don't have a computer problem. We still have a leadership problem. You can't lead with your father pulling in another direction. His very presence in Scottsville is an impediment to your leadership. On Friday, we're going to do what we need to do. We're going to force him off the board. In fact, we think he should move out of his office in Scottsville."

"Look," I said, "in January his older son fired his younger son. In July, his wife and lifelong sweetheart died. And now, doing this in November could kill him."

"It's time for you to put family second," he said. "You can't lead under these circumstances. You've got to have a new priority here. You've got a bigger family to take care of now."

"Well, I can't let him walk into a surprise. I have to go to Scottsville and tell him."

At that point, Wallace began writing on a sheet of paper. He handed it to me and said, "This is his resignation. Get him to sign it."

My heart was as heavy as it had ever been when I got to Scottsville the next morning. Ironically, my dad was sitting in Steve's old office, at Steve's desk, when I walked in. He lit up as he always did when I came into a room, full of love and affection for me.

"Hi, Son," he said, a big smile on his face.

I couldn't even say hello. I just put the paper in front of him. He read it, signed it, and said, "Now you can tell Bruce Quinnell to go to hell."

I had been driven to the meeting by a new, young driver, who waited out front during that painful father-son encounter. I practically dragged myself back into the passenger seat, and the driver turned to me and said, "So, are you going to have a good Christmas this year?"

I couldn't respond. I cleared my throat and said, "Our next stop is my sister's house."

I said to Laura Jo, "Daddy really needs you now, and I'm here to tell you why." After I went through my encounter with him, Laura Jo's comment was, "I sure hate problems that don't have solutions."

When I arrived in Nashville, I had a call from Laura Jo, who said, "Daddy has requested that you tear up his resignation." I immediately said okay, but when I relayed the message to Wallace Rasmussen, he said, "Nothing doing. That resignation is an official record of the company now." I realized that he was right. I had to put family second.

On Friday, my dad put off going to the board meeting until finally we got someone to drive him down from Scottsville. It was the toughest meeting I've ever attended. The sight of him as he walked into the boardroom will haunt me all my life. My father, my mentor, my number one sponsor, my dear friend, was a different person. He was broken, defeated. He looked as bad as I felt. Steve, who was still on the board, was in the room as well—it was a pitiful family gathering. The fact that he had called me and stood with me when I fired Steve made it that much harder for me to support the board's stand against him. He was forced by the board to retire as chairman but they relented and he was allowed to remain on the board. Essentially he had been put on notice to behave. The directive that he move out of his office remained, but I would make sure it wasn't put into effect. Still, the damage had been done. I became chairman during the meeting. Nothing had ever felt less like a promotion!

After the meeting, we issued a press release stating that Cal Sr. was retiring from active management, effective December 31, but that he would remain a member of the board.

With Mama gone, Steve fired, and my dad forced out as chairman, neither the company nor the family would ever feel the same again. That Christmas, my dad, my brother and sisters, and their families made plans for the family get-together in Scottsville. I called my dad and said, "I assume that it is best for Margaret, Calister, and me not to come up for Christmas." He cleared his throat and said,

"I think that's right." We spent a long and lonely Christmas in Nashville, away from the family and the first family holiday gathering without my mother at its center.

After the first of the year, my dad gathered a little resolve. Under Kentucky law, he still had the votes to fire outside directors, and he wanted two of the four gone. "Larry Appley has to go," he said. "Nothing's been right in this company since that SOB showed up. I want to fire him. Wallace Rasmussen too."

There was no use arguing about Larry—he had already taught us a great deal about strategic planning, and he was in his eighties—but it was important that we hang on to Wallace.

"Daddy," I said, "Wallace Rasmussen is chairman of the audit committee. He's known to be one of the best in that capacity, and he's been on the board for less than a year."

"I don't care," he said. "I don't like how he talked to me."

"Daddy," I said, "that's not good enough. If I can't determine my own board of directors as CEO, then I think I'm going to have to resign."

His eyes filled with tears, and I watched as one rolled down his cheek.

"Son, it would devastate my lifelong dream to see anybody but you as CEO of this company. And I hope you don't do that when I fire Wallace Rasmussen!"

It was quite apparent he was deadly serious and that we were two bull elephants facing off. He had the legal authority to fire two directors. I could have renominated them and gotten them reelected at a separate special shareholders' meeting afterward, but that would amount to a huge spectacle. There was no sense in airing our dirty linen publicly. I decided to nominate two other directors to replace them.

I knew, though, that we had to hang on to Wallace, so I announced at the shareholders' meeting that the turnaround required such a concentration of effort that Wallace Rasmussen was going to come off the board and become a management development consultant. That would allow him to dedicate the necessary time and energy to his work for the company and to have more involvement than is appropriate for a director.

Wallace accepted, and we slowly—very slowly—started the turnaround we so desperately needed. Wallace was also able to rebuild a bridge to my dad, making two trips to Scottsville to talk to him.

"Mr. Turner, I have to tell you," he said at one point, "if I had been Cal Turner and had gone through all that you have gone through, I wouldn't have handled myself nearly as well as you did."

I honestly think my dad would have preferred that Wallace not be so nice to him. I believe he gradually got to the point where he was saying, "No, I can't hate this man."

A year and a half after it all happened, my dad said, "Okay, Wallace can come back on the board. I think he has learned his lesson." With Wallace back in place, we were positioned for the nineties, a period of explosive growth for us.

My dad and I would have only one more big disagreement, and that was over the firing of the only district manager (out of 125) to fail a random drug test. We had a drug-free policy, and I knew he should be fired. His father, though, was my dad's favorite operations employee and my dad said, "You're not going to fire him. His father has done more for this company than all of your senior management team put together."

I fired him, but the fight convinced me we couldn't keep going through this. I needed to make my dad behave if at all possible. I knew the company was his baby, and that he loved it as he loved family; that helped me come up with a plan. I went to Scottsville again and said, "Daddy, our family's been through a lot of pain. I don't want any more fights, but these things keep coming up. Every time, it tears my heart out. I know my siblings wouldn't want to sell their stock unless I sold mine, so why don't we agree that the whole Turner family will sell Dollar General? Let's get our family back."

I knew what he was going to say. He'd be flabbergasted. "No," he'd tell me. "Then here's what I need from you," I'd say, and I'd convince him to stay out of things.

Well, I finished my spiel, making my pitch for selling the company, and he said, "Okay."

I was the one who was flabbergasted. "Okay?" I said. "Well, I'll have to share this with my management team. We need them to get the company in good enough shape to sell, and I'll suggest they go to the board with a bonus and compensation plan that would reward them upon a successful sale of the company."

They came back with something I considered far too lucrative, but the board surprised me and approved it. With the carrot of big incentive pay and a real ownership stake dangling before them, they took this turnaround that had been so slow in getting started and kicked it into overdrive. The team came together and we were off on the best run in the company's history. Soon it was apparent that Dollar General was the kind of company none of us, management or family, would want to sell. My bluff backfired in the best way possible, and we remained owners of a company that prospered greatly. It was one of the most productive changes the company underwent in my entire career.

It had begun with family turmoil, with a company being pulled in three directions. I had to reach as deeply as I've ever reached to discover my greatest value, the one that trumps all the others when I have to make a decision. I had to see if I had what it took to be decisive, to do what I thought best for the company, to direct that misplaced wedding vow, "I do," at my brother, and take him out of the picture. It was a matter of seeing that the company had gotten bigger than our family, and that it needed more expertise and resolve than we could bring to it *as* a family.

If we hadn't gotten in trouble, we never would have grappled with the bigger questions that led us to better, more professional management. Ultimately, though, that had played out with my brother leaving the company and my father forced into an advisory role. Ironically, my brother would be made wealthy by the success of a management team he was no longer part of, and he and I are closer today than we have ever been because, although it was the hardest thing I've ever done in my life, it was the right thing to do.

And he was prophetic—I still feel the scars of it. And yes, I will live with it the rest of my life.

There was, during that long season of turmoil, a development that spawned a wonderful family legacy. It grew out of our recognition that the company's charitable efforts were haphazard. Local organizations from Little League teams to the United Way approached individual store managers, who did what they could, using their own judgment as to what was effective and appropriate. By the mid-eighties, the company had grown so large, we realized this was too random and ineffective an approach. It only made sense for Dollar General to choose a cause or causes and attempt to make a collective difference, something that offered a long-term boost to those we served.

We looked at our customers and their communities. Both were often rural and isolated. The people had limited incomes and skill sets. Through it all ran a lack of educational opportunities. We knew that some of our customers had reading difficulties and that some were illiterate. We knew, too, that some of our employees had never finished high school. They would need help in getting ahead.

Our research turned up statistics that put what we saw into national perspective. Many of the states served by Dollar General were on the leading edge of a disastrous trend that saw 850,000 students drop out of school each year while just 450,000 were earning GEDs.

The best thing we could do, we thought, was to support literacy programs, something that definitely hit home with us. Luther Turner had succeeded despite a third-grade education—or perhaps because of his ability to turn his lack of education into a lifelong willingness to learn from others. Our cause became the terrible gaps in education, income, and opportunity that afflicted so many DG customers. We decided we would do whatever we could to further literacy, especially economic literacy, among those customers and our employees.

We began in 1986 by picking up the cost of GED study materials and test fees for our employees. Meanwhile, we talked to national adult education officials, who told us that many agencies existed to help but that people were often discouraged or intimidated by the process of tracking down and accessing information. They might make several long-distance calls to a state government office, only to be sent to another and another. If they did reach the right agency, they might wait weeks for information on programs offered in their communities.

We were in those communities and we decided to help get that information to them, quickly and at our expense. In 1987, we launched our Learn to Read Information Program. A customer could pick up a preaddressed reply card at one of our stores, mail it to our home office, and receive information about the closest adult education office. We devoted half a million dollars' worth of our paid retail advertising to encouraging customers to go to their nearest DG store for help, and 375 radio stations devoted over $200,000 in air time to assist the program. We put 300,000 brochures in circulation. In the first year, nearly 6,000 people in twenty-eight states requested information.

The government noticed, and in 1988, we were one of thirty organizations receiving the Presidential Citation for Private Sector Initiatives from Ronald Reagan.

But statistics and citations don't tell the story. Hearing a man in his sixties say that he came to us wanting more than anything to be able to write a love note to his wife, or having another tell us how he had once shied away from any attention out of shame that he couldn't read or write, and being able to overcome that—those were the stories that let us know we were doing something worthwhile.

As a corporation, we contributed money. As an individual, I wanted to know more about the problem, and I talked about it with Nelson Andrews, a friend who was on the board of First American Bank with me. I was interested in education as it was playing out in local schools, since that was where our next generation of leaders was going to come from. Nelson had his finger on that pulse, as he had on so many. He was a community leader, someone who reached out and genuinely tried to make life better for others. He had done a lot of work in education and he challenged me, saying, "Cal, if you presume to understand the problems of education and literacy, you need to spend a full day in an inner-city classroom. And I mean you need to be there when the teacher gets there, you need to go through everything she experiences, and you need to leave when she does. There's too much about the educational problem you're not going to understand unless you do."

I agreed that it was a good idea, and Nelson arranged for me to spend the day with fourth graders at a school in Nashville. I arrived at 7:00 and met with the teacher before the students came in. As they did, she told me a little about each one.

"So and so had a bad night," she'd say. She told me that most had only one parent and some didn't know where that one was. Some wanted to spend the night in the classroom because they were afraid they'd get shot at home. It was terrible, terrible stuff, and it was a major effort just to get their attention so we could proceed with some instruction. As a manager, I would say that it was the most unmanageable situation I had ever encountered, but it was good for me because I became sympathetic about the problems that teachers have. It's easy to blame them for our bad educational system, but I learned that many of the students they deal with every day come to school with so many problems and so much dysfunction at home that they are often simply not ready to meet the challenges the classroom presents.

The teacher assigned me to work especially with a boy named Tony, saying he could use a little extra help and attention. I talked to him a lot through the course of the day, and he really warmed up to me. He could tell I cared about him and his classmates, and I could see that he admired and respected this adult who was there trying to encourage him. At one point, late in the day, he asked me if I was rich. I was embarrassed. The thought of being rich has always embarrassed me. I said no.

I knew when I said it that I was being dishonest. To this day, I think I blew it. If I had said yes, he would have gotten the idea that being rich didn't automatically mean you're a bad person. He might even have gotten the idea that if he worked hard, he could someday be a rich person himself. There were dots I wish I'd connected for him during a day that taught me a great deal—and that didn't end when the students left at 3:00. I stayed there with the teacher until she finished up between 5:00 and 5:30 p.m.

The other development in the wake of our family's turmoil was, paradoxically enough, the most impressive period of success in our history. The outcome of the crisis—a new, independent board and a much stronger management team—had led us into a new era. Still, the twin realities of my dad's ouster as chairman and his continued presence on the board were indicative of the dichotomy at the heart of Dollar General as we entered the 1990s. Our legacy was small-town but we were headquartered in Nashville. We were small neighborhood stores and we were a *Fortune* 500 company. We had moved from entrepreneurial chaos to strategic planning, from family rule to an independent board, but we were very much a mix of two worlds.

Part of splitting the difference, I thought, was my continuing effort to bring a personal touch to my leadership. It's why I had a column every month in our company newsletter, and why it was often of a personal nature. I'd talk shop, explain policies, reminisce, and try to let everyone in the company know he or she was appreciated, often using personal anecdotes to bring the point home.

Dollar General was constantly changing, growing and adapting in an evolving marketplace, and part of what I wanted to do was to make change attractive. I hit on the notion of Sacred Cals, statements that summed up the old company culture and which might—or might not—need skewering. Based on the fact that Cal Turner and his summations of policy were pretty much sacrosanct, my willingness to talk about slaughtering Sacred Cals was just the kind of attention-grabbing irreverence that let me set the right tone while making important points. It was a logical extension of the self-effacing management style I'd used since the beginning, and since I was a Cal Turner, too, I could include myself in the Sacred Cals. All the while, I was making clear our commitment to change and the fact that I was personally excited by it. I was asking everyone to join me in making change happen based on the right foundation.

One example involved packing trailers for shipment, something I'd done since I was a kid. As we got into logistics, I held it as a principle—a Sacred Cal—that the trailers had to be "cubed out." If you had packed all the merchandise going to one store into the trailer and had room left over, whether it was six feet or twenty feet, you started on the next store's stuff. You'd pack until that trailer was full, then start on the nose of the next one. The principle was maximum utilization of space. Underneath that was the notion that you didn't want to be hauling air from one place to another. "Cube out every trailer" was a Sacred Cal if there ever was one, which meant it

if you just set out to make money. Success, in other words, is about relationships.

- *Don't hire anyone who doesn't walk fast.* My dad could not stand to see people idle or dawdling.
- *Don't describe the labor pains. Show me the baby.* He didn't want long-winded speeches or meetings either. This was another way to say, *Don't be plan planners. Be plan doers.*

There were a couple of Sacred Cals left over from Luther Turner as well:

- *Always plow to the end of the row.* Finish a job before you take on another.
- *A mule is smarter than a man, because once a mule learns his stall in the barn, he'll always return to it. A man forgets his stall.* "Oh, I can get into this other business," or "I'm tired of what I do well. I'll move on to something else." That one has an offshoot: *Being good at this doesn't mean I'm good at that.* When I understand my core competence, I also understand my core weakness. That will enable me to know what I need to surround myself with in terms of people and talent.

My dad had Sacred Cals in the personal realm as well:

- *Marry a woman who lives where you want to live, because that's where you will live.*
- *Son, anytime you meet a man who says he's the boss at home, don't believe anything else he says.*

In keeping with our approach to Sacred Cals, I looked at my father's ground rules for employees: *Work hard. Be honest. Don't drink on the job. Don't screw the help.* They were that simple, or that simplistic. Those were in essence childhood rules. I wanted to bring adult rules to bear on the company. Childhood rules work from the outside. Adult rules work from the inside. Childhood rules are a great starting point, and you can't get to adult rules unless you understand the more fundamental childhood rules, but just as a child has to move from external coercion to internal guidance to reach adulthood, a company has to encourage its people to be guided by the internal rather than the external. Those childhood rules became another Sacred Cal.

We put that approach in motion by encouraging each executive to apply the principles of strategic planning on a personal level. Our executive training included the process of helping and encouraging each executive to arrive at an individual values statement and working from there.

On a company basis, we looked at the way we made decisions as well. There is always the risk that management will get out of touch with the realities of life in the stores, so we tried to require that before any instructional memo went out to the stores, its author had to take the action it suggested and successfully implement it *in a store.* Once it was proven to work, it could be put on paper and mailed out. It was in keeping with our notion that the real genius in the company lay with the employees in the stores, because they were in closest contact with customers and day-to-day problems. Nevertheless, that was somehow one of those rules we were not always able to follow!

All of that helped us deal with a retailing landscape that had by the 1990s changed dramatically. Many of the old giants had disappeared or were in trouble. Wal-Mart had grown in twenty-five years from 1 to 1,200 stores—and since we studied everything, we knew that sales in DG stores were better if they were within a mile of a Wal-Mart, since Wal-Mart chose great locations and drew even more customers to the area. Many of the chains that had followed our example were flourishing. Still, when retailers gathered, you could hear many of them complain about the fact that there was no more customer loyalty. The way I looked at it, customers grant loyalty when retailers earn it, and it has to be earned every day. I always thought that when a retailer began complaining about customer loyalty, he had somehow fallen short of *earning* that loyalty.

Our customers had always been very smart. They had to be, given their struggles. They weren't as sold on brand loyalty. They weren't as interested in keeping up with the Joneses. They were struggling to keep up with life. At a time when it took two paychecks to keep families afloat, people paid attention to economics. We knew the best thing we could do was to dig more deeply into our founding concept. Dollar pricing meant you could check customers out quickly; small stores were less intimidating and they made it easy to keep up with what was selling and keep track of inventory; and since we were selling basics, we were not as vulnerable to changing fashions as other merchants. We knew economics would always force low-income customers to know value and we knew there was a real niche in retailing for a low-cost provider of basics—things people use up and buy when they run out, such as soap, shampoo, toothpaste, and the like. People don't replace their toilet seats very often. They replace their toilet *paper* frequently! We wanted to be in stock on it and all the other basics when our customers ran out of them. Most retailers at one point or another fall prey to the temptation to upgrade. They start with an eye to value but then bring in higher-priced goods with bigger markups. In times of economic stress, the middle market produces a lot of corpses. We were fortunate in our stubborn determination to stay at the low end and serve the low-income customer. There would be no French perfume, designer dresses, or diamond-studded dog collars. My father had always kept it simple.

"Value is what it's all about," he said. "Getting what you pay for, knowing what you're buying, and finding what you're looking for."

It worked. For Dollar General, the nineties started with a bang. The company was reenergized, in large part due to the incentive plan we put in place when we thought we'd be selling the company. Our bonus package for managers dated back to the first Dollar General store in 1955, but once we started strategic planning, we began talking about expanding that to include the senior management group, the people charged with growing the company. We had to figure out a way to measure the effectiveness of the strategic initiatives they undertook, and ultimately we decided it should be company performance as reflected in profitability—return on assets. If we were performing for the shareholders, we would get a bonus. It seemed to be a great way to ensure teamwork and cooperation, providing an incentive to lower that all-important cost-to-sales ratio. Perhaps most important, compensation would not be targeted to individuals; group performance would be the key as we sought to include as much of management as possible in what amounted to real ownership in the company.

I viewed a lot of this through the lens of my life as a practicing, backsliding Methodist, which let me evolve my own take on what my dad said: "I only expect the competition to do everything it can to me."

People are basically self-centered, looking out for their own interests. It's built into us as a survival mechanism. Still, it's an instinct we need to overcome, and the way to get over human selfishness is first to see that we all have it and to forgive one another, and then to recognize that all of us are in need of help and cooperation. We can turn that innate selfishness to good by helping one another to attain mutual success.

Collaboration, then, is the process of raising individual selfishness to group cooperation and accomplishment, which can spur the group—or the organization, the nation, or the planet—to greater success.

In our case, we needed to recognize that meeting our customers' needs and wants was our key to success. Everyone in the company had to pull in the same direction to get that done. Our employee stock option program encouraged us to do just that, and it was showing remarkable results. Sometime in 1991, I was talking to one of our field persons about our obvious success and he said, "There are two reasons—our stores carry the basics at the right price, and all our people have stock options." A year later, we expanded and formalized our profit sharing under a program called Teamshare. It extended both profit sharing and stock options to store managers and assistant store managers with at least two years on the job—managers would have 150 shares under option and assistant managers 100. That more than doubled the pool of employees with performance-based stock options, to 6,500. As far as I knew, we were the only retail company to do that. Not all of the managers even knew what stock options were, so I used the newsletter column to attempt an explanation:

A share of stock is an ownership stake in the company and its profits. Its price reflects the health of the company—generally, as the company does well, its stock price rises. Granting a stock option—the right to purchase a given number of shares at a set price—is a means of extending company ownership. The option is available at that same price for a period that may not expire for years. If the stock rises, that option becomes more valuable, as you may be able to buy for $10 a stock that is now worth $20— so there's a great incentive to work hard to make the company more successful, as reflected in a higher stock price.

My hope was always that the prospect of wealth would become the prospect of serving others in a deeper and better way, because they are one and the same. Success is based on satisfied customers. It was only if we could truly deliver on our mission of giving them a better life that the company would succeed enough to make all the holders of DG stock options rich.

At the same time, we were pouring thought and money into our warehouses, spending $17 million to streamline distribution. We redesigned our Homerville, Georgia, facility and converted the one in Scottsville from manual operation to automation, completing a $9.8-million warehouse known as Building 8, which featured state-of-the-art distribution equipment including computer-operated conveyor belts, bar-coded shipping labels, and "starburst" laser scanners. We were now shipping to ninety-six stores from twenty-four loading docks in Scottsville alone. We added fifty-three employees and worked them hard—the amount of overtime in Scottsville and Homerville jumped from 15,000 hours to 82,500 in one year. We also added seven new buyers, two merchandise managers, and a director of merchandise administration. What's more, in spite of the aggressive agenda of change, total employee turnover dropped by 15 percent.

In 1992, we doubled the size of the Homerville center at an additional cost of $9 million, and gradually we opened up new distribution centers in Ardmore, Oklahoma, and South Boston, Virginia. We would soon invest $7 million in automated cash registers for all our stores as well.

Behind those facts and figures lay the reality that the early nineties represented a sea change in the way we sent out merchandise. When I say we were converting our warehouses from "manual operation," I mean people had been pushing two-wheelers around inside the buildings, wondering where things were. It was a "best guess" operation, since they didn't know what the stores really needed and were scared to rely on managers to order the correct items and quantities.

Our new buyers were looking at customer pull, not buyer push, in line with the approach we had undertaken since our first implementation of strategic planning. New technology in the form of a MARS ordering system let us keep track of precisely what was selling store by store, and the buyers set about "creaming the lines" to figure out the 20 percent of each category of merchandise that generated 80 percent of the sales. That's what we had to be stocking. Then it was a matter of keeping merchandise flowing to the stores on a frequent and predictable basis. We had hoped to be moving 50,000 to 60,000 cartons a day out of Scottsville in the wake of these improvements, and it actually turned out to be over 100,000. We had come a long way since the days when store managers took out the backseats of their cars so we could stuff a lot of whatever we had into them.

Then there was shrinkage. Merchandise is going to disappear. Our problem had settled down quite a bit since the days after we'd taken on the Eagle stores in Florida, but at one point in 1991, the head of operations and merchandising came to me saying it had gotten bad again.

"The loss prevention department wants more money so it can do more of what it's doing," he said, "but it's obvious it isn't working. I'm wondering if we shouldn't have them do *less* of what they're doing. Why don't we cut back on that department?"

He was obviously proud of what amounted to a counterintuitive suggestion. I thought it was a great idea. In fact, I didn't think it went far enough.

"I appreciate your thought," I said, "and I accept it completely. In fact, let's just eliminate the loss prevention department."

His expression was priceless. He never expected me to push *less* to *zero*. It made sense, though. Let's say a store was losing a lot of merchandise and the best guess was that it was an employee. The store manager would call loss prevention and they might send in some-body from a shopping service to catch the dishonest employee. Then the loss prevention people would come in and get the confession, which would be turned over to a district manager, who would come in and do the firing. Now, the clerk knows he's going to be fired, but there's a delay until the district manager can get there to make it official, so he's got days or even a couple of weeks to steal more, with nothing more to lose. In the meantime, you have to hire a replace-ment, and since you're doing it quickly, you don't have time for a thorough screening, so you might end up with someone who's just as dishonest.

Overall, that's addressing the symptom, not the disease. Playing cops and robbers is not loss prevention. It's dealing with loss on the back end rather than the front end. So why not let the operators—the manager and assistant manager, backed up by the district manager—take charge of the total operation of that store, includ-ing loss control? You're bringing accountability closer to the action, so you should be more effective in controlling it. In this case, we made it clear that shrinkage affected bonuses. If they could stop it at the store level, their year-end checks would be larger. We figured that would inspire sufficient self-policing to make a difference. The clerks would report a manager who was stealing goods just as readily as a manager would report a clerk. So that's what we did. Above all, we made it clear that the best thing they could do as operators was to make sure we hired the right people in the first place, then make sure the operating culture was right.

And it worked. Our shrinkage-to-sales ratio dropped from 3.1 percent in 1991 to 2.4 percent a year later—without a loss prevention department!

The early nineties also saw four straight years of double-digit same-store gains. Six-month figures ending July 31, 1993, showed a

46.9 percent leap in earnings on a sales increase of 17.7 percent, to $477.4 million. Net sales for the fiscal year were well over $900 million, up 22 percent. Net income was $36.5 million, up a remarkable 65.4 percent. The company whose economic growth once prompted my dad to whisper to his father that we had passed a million dollars in profit was now approaching a billion dollars in sales.

Just as financial incentives for employees fed those increases, the increases fed employee compensation across the board. The Turners, of course, benefited greatly from all this. Although I had long recognized the great gap between the lives of the Turners and people like that poor old farmer buying panties for his wife when I was a teenage sales clerk, I never felt rich until sometime after the company had moved to Nashville in 1986. We had always been conservative in terms of the salaries we had drawn from the company. In fact, I remember my sister Laura Jo asking me to come out to her house in Scottsville once.

"Cal Jr.," she said, "when will the company ever pay my husband a living wage?"

"Laura Jo," I said, "I don't know." That was just the way my dad was.

I remember talking to her husband, Wayne, many years later and saying, "Wayne, do you know that when I came out of the Navy and went to work for my dad, I took a cut in pay?"

Wayne, with his rich Southern accent, said, "Cal Juniah, when I came to work for your fathah, I also took a cut in pay. And I had been a schoolteachah."

In the wake of all that had happened, that was no longer the case.

That left one member of the family looking at a possible career. My son, Calister, had worked in Dollar General stores during high school, and of course he was steeped in the culture, as I had been when I was young. He also knew the turmoil the family had been through in the late eighties, and that I didn't want him to go through that. I had told him I didn't want him to join the company. Still, one day he said, "Dad, I love Dollar General. If there is a job available in the company I'd be qualified for, is it all right if I apply?" I said, "Before you even apply, I want you to discuss it with me." There might have been something in my voice that nailed down what he knew of my sentiments, because that was the end of that. He never talked about working for Dollar General again, and he went on to make his own mark in Nashville.

At about that time, I received one of the biggest shocks of my life. My dad called me into his office one day and said, "Son, I need to tell you something. I don't want you to think ill of me if you ever take a look at my estate and you can't figure out what happened to the nine million dollars I got from our public offering in 1971."

That was the deal my dad had called off and then restarted. It baffled me at the time, but I'd just let it go after he adamantly declined to answer my questions. I hadn't thought about that $9 million since the deal, but now, of course, my ears perked up.

He paused. "In truth," he said, "at that time Mr. Guy Comer owned half of our company. He and I had a letter of agreement on the side signed by both of us."

Guy Comer had owned Washington Manufacturing Company in Nashville. They made overalls, then jeans, and later sportswear. He was a good friend of my dad's and a father figure to him from the early days of the company. I remember their getting together to talk about business at our house, but I had no idea he owned half the company. This was completely out of the blue.

My dad said that in the late fifties, he wanted to carry many of the goods Mr. Comer was manufacturing. They worked up a deal where Mr. Comer would provide quite a lot of them in exchange for half the company. They never told anyone—they didn't even bring in a lawyer. They drew up a simple agreement and signed it. All of the common stock was issued to Turner family members when we went public, and no one but my father and Mr. Comer knew that he owned half of it. I was the one talking to Wall Street analysts and the SEC, and I had no idea of the true state of our ownership. My dad knew I would have been unable to function with that knowledge, so he kept it from me. If I'd known, I would have been guilty of falsifying statements, and the ramifications would have been huge.

Mr. Comer died in 1969, and as they were settling his estate, his management called my dad and asked to meet with him. My dad took his personal accountant, Ed Lynch, to the meeting because no one at Dollar General knew anything about this. Mr. Comer's board told my dad they wanted to sell their half of the company and they gave him their high asking price.

"Well," said my dad, "you'll notice in that letter of agreement that Mr. Guy and I signed, that the partner who wanted out could name the price and the other partner could decide whether to buy or to sell at that price. You've named your price and I congratulate you. You have just bought the other half of Dollar General." With that, he walked out of the meeting. Ed followed him and said, "Cal, what just happened in there? They bought your company!"

"No, they didn't," said my dad. "They don't know what to do with the company. They can't run it."

Sure enough, it wasn't long before he got a phone call from Washington Manufacturing Company's Paul Hargis.

"Cal," he said. "We can't buy the company."

"I know you can't," said my dad.

"So why don't you come in and let's talk about what we can work out," Paul said.

Washington Manufacturing brought the price down and my dad bought them out. That's where the $9 million from our issuance of stock had gone.

15

❦

Serving Others: A Mission That Mattered

We learned the lessons of strategic planning and the applications of mission statements as we went, and one of the key lessons was that neither was worth much unless it had a positive impact on the culture and operations of the company. That was true for all of our constituencies. When it came to our bosses, the persons who believed in us enough to put their retirement funds at risk in our stock, we were committed to delivering not just great results, but superior return on their investment. Making that happen for shareholders depended on our other critically important constituencies: our employees and our customers.

Tying it all together was the phrase "Serving Others," and in 1993, we revisited our mission statement, expanding it to make clear how "Serving Others" impacted every constituent group. It read:

Our Mission—Serving Others

- Our customers...with greatest everyday value.
- Our shareholders...with superior return on investment.
- Our employees...as partners in total development.

For employees, the mission of Serving Others colored everything done at work. In keeping with a truth of the retailing business that dated back before the first Turner store existed and is in effect to this day, our employees worked long and hard, but those grueling store hours were essential to serving our customers with the greatest everyday value, which was our opportunity to help give them a better life. Furthermore, Serving Others, rather than self, is our opportunity to partner with fellow employees to accomplish their total development.

Most of those employees were women. I think retailing done as Serving Others has a feminine quality, a mothering dynamic. A store becomes a "home" to customers, a place where they are always welcome. When they go in, they are greeted in a way that says, "You are special." They are given concerned, caring attention. Of course the store is clean and neat and the prices are low. The mothering dynamic also includes toughness and hard work. Housekeeping and storekeeping involve lots of work that must be done over and over, and the personal requirements of both are love, patience, and sweat.

Given the family dynamics of the company, one of the criticisms directed at us really stung. We got plenty of letters in those days about the fact that on Sundays and holidays, we closed our offices and distribution centers but not our stores. Christmas and Easter were the only days the stores closed.

"Why," people would write, "does a retail organization with spiritual and family values not honor the majority of its employees with much-deserved time off on Sundays and holidays?" Frankly, the subject always bothered me. Those letters began almost as soon as we opened our stores for business on Sundays in 1988, and a lot of those letters came from ministers. My reply to them was aggressive.

"Reverend Jones," I would write, "I share your regret about our stores being open on Sunday, but, unfortunately, the majority of your congregation wants to shop with us on Sunday. Until you can change their minds about that from the pulpit, we will have to keep our stores open on Sunday. May your ministry become more effective!"

I have to admit that I now feel bad about that answer, particularly since I had seriously considered the ministry and should not have criticized the effectiveness of anyone called to preach. I always felt bad about our store employees having to work on Sundays and holidays, but giving our customers better lives and honoring our shareholders' investment required our stores to be open and selling consumable basics anytime our customers needed them, and we encouraged employees, who did not routinely work seven days a week, to have lives balanced in work, recreation, and leisure.

What I said at the time was, "Perhaps there is a greater blessing in ministering to mankind on Sundays or holidays than in ministering to self or even to family."

There were other policies that fit with the family's attitude about business. For one, we never took credit cards back then. My dad had always been against it, and I inherited his disdain for them. Credit cards would have worked against the simple, value-oriented nature of our concept. Our whole business was built on the simplicity of the cash transaction at the store for items we sold at the lowest possible prices. Our customers visited us frequently and bought just what they needed at the time of need, and it was all cash. In those days, credit card companies charged about 3 percent on each transaction, and that was our net profit margin. We did not want to charge our customers more or have to hire more people at our headquarters to deal with the credit card companies and all the related paperwork and expense.

But we used to hear about it now and then. My friend Martha Ingram, a Nashvillian who in 1995 became chairman and CEO of Ingram Industries and who was known for her commitment to and generosity toward the arts community, had a summer home in the Blue Ridge Mountains of North Carolina. One day she went to our store in the town of Cashiers to stock up. She came to the checkout with a shopping cart full of stuff and offered the clerk her credit card.

"We don't take credit cards," the cashier told her.

She pulled out her checkbook, and when the clerk saw she was from Tennessee, she said, "We don't take out-of-state checks."

"Well," Martha said, "is it okay if I put my cart to the side here and find an ATM and get cash?" and the cashier assured her it was.

Not long afterward, she said to me, "So much for the thought that we live in a paperless society."

The next year, as she was getting ready to go back to the mountains, she said, "Cal, are you going to take my credit card this year?"

"No," I said, "to tell you the truth, we're not, Martha, but we're working on debit cards so we can accept your food stamps."

Fortunately, she had a good laugh about that.

That and all the other cost-cutting moves we undertook as a matter of principle continued to pay off. In 1993, our operating cost as a percentage of sales was down from 23.6 to 22.4 percent, and I was starting to think 20 percent was possible. I hadn't announced it or committed to it yet, but I thought I would indeed make it a goal soon enough.

By now everyone had caught on to the kind of roll we were on. Dollar General stock appreciated 66 percent in 1993 alone, hitting a record high of 34¾ on September 29. We were roaring. In 1994, we opened 302 stores, and we planned to open at least as many in 1995.

In the fall of 1994, senior management took a week to make plans for the next five years. The excitement was electric. We were convinced we could keep the spectacular growth trends of the first half of the nineties going through the second half. We did feel that we needed a statement of strategy to guide our entire team, and in looking over our progress, we agreed that our system of rewards spurred people to do their best work. Since we hadn't micromanaged that, we didn't need to start now. We didn't want control interfering with the performance of good people wanting to demonstrate what they could do. It went back to my childhood, where my mother gave us values that would serve us far better than restrictive controls. She believed in us and we developed belief in ourselves. It was the most productive growth influence we could have had. It's the way I wanted to position the company, moving from my dad's external controls to a values-based internal dynamic. The statement we came up with was this: "The least control for the most development of our niche." The statement of company values, also rewritten that week, included this sentence: "We believe that productivity is attained by emphasizing strengths in a positive environment, not by dwelling on weaknesses in an environment of guilt and blame." Set people in motion with values and a mission, we reasoned, and let them do what they do best.

I summed up our approach to a reporter this way: "We are trying to be a neighborhood store that is customer-friendly, that is one smooth-functioning unit of a distribution network. We distribute the basics to low-income people. We don't run sales or stress fashion. At Christmas, our best-selling item might be toilet paper."

It wasn't glamorous, but it worked. Analysts loved us.

"Dollar General has become so feverish in keeping its prices down," said Craig Weichmann of Morgan Keegan & Company, "they are emerging as the price leader in the community. In their overwhelming success the last five years, they truly have passed on savings to the consumer and consumers have rewarded them with strong sales growth." Weichmann cited a discount-store price survey in which he found DG's prices on sampled products to be 5 to 10 percent *below* Wal-Mart's.

The year 1995 tempered our optimism a bit, as our growth was slower, although still solid. In January 1996, we planned on giving out the fourth straight payout under our Teamshare profit-sharing program for executives, store managers, and assistant managers. But it turned out there were ways to game the system, something that's just a fact of business life. All at once we could tell there were excessive claims charging nonexistent markdowns to the warehouse, then selling the merchandise at full price. We'd been lenient and they were taking advantage of us. On March 19, 1996, I sent a memo to store managers and district managers announcing a Teamshare bonus adjustment as the result of slowed sales. When it became clear that it was even worse than we thought, I announced that Teamshare bonuses would be withdrawn altogether, something that affected office and distribution center employees as well as store employees.

I got lobbied hard on that one, and after a bit of internal debate, I changed my mind.

"Our system created some real problems and some employees took advantage of that," I said. "I didn't want them to take advantage of other employees and shareholders, but I realized there is no way to make this come out right without hurting a lot of good, loyal, hard-working employees. The decision cost $1.3 million and will reward a few dishonest people."

We put into place tightened security measures when it came to processing deliveries, and resisted calls for accepting credit cards, which the company didn't do until 2003, a year after I left. Taken together, all of those cost-cutting measures, combined with record sales, helped boost us pretty quickly right back into record territory.

Throughout my years with the company, our realized gross profit margin ranged between 23 and 29 percent. It never hit 30. Our competition was generally in the 30s, and part of the reason lay in our different approaches. Our competitors had a broader assortment of merchandise and greater markups to cover their higher expenses. Our focus was on a limited assortment and low everyday prices. Keeping a tight rein on costs, we kept bringing operating expenses down. Finally, in fact, we set that goal of bringing them under 20 percent of sales. We were running a pretty tight ship in most areas, and I'd even been rethinking advertising, which at one time amounted to 3.6 percent of sales, or more than $100 million per year.

Advertising wasn't the necessity it would seem to be, and it actually gave us problems. Our stores were scattered in small towns over a wide area, which made it difficult for us to get every item offered in a direct-mail sales brochure out of our warehouses, into our trucks, and out to every store by a printed sales deadline. And if an item proved to be especially popular, we never seemed to have enough of it in stores. Customers got frustrated. They'd show up and we'd have to give them rain checks. More often we'd ship merchandise that wouldn't sell completely and we'd have the cost of unsold inventory plus the cost of all those trucks rolling and warehouses hustling to get goods out into the stores. Then our trucks would be so loaded with sale merchandise that we sometimes wouldn't have room to ship the basics. I thought, *Wait a minute! Why can't we be the one retailer with the guts to stop this advertising madness?* We could eliminate that 3.6 percent of cost against sales, lower our prices, and give better value to the customers. We would also be more consistently in stock on everyday items because the trucks wouldn't be full of advertised goods. And lower costs would mean lower everyday prices—which was what we were all about.

I got input from everybody, and I can't say anybody saw it completely the way I did. Nobody in our business operated without this kind of advertising. My mind was made up, though. We'd been running company-wide circulars for years—as many as thirteen of them in a year—but our best advertising was word-of-mouth and I was convinced it was all we needed. We went through withdrawal each time we decided not to print a company-wide circular and we took short-term sales hits—up to 30 or 40 percent at first—but I was confident that using that money to lower prices would boost sales in the long run. In 1993, we printed just five circulars, and we gradually got the number down to two, and then to zero. In the process, we lowered our advertising costs from 3.6 percent to less than .25 percent.

Sales bounced back quickly and soon outpaced what we'd been

doing. By 1997, with advertising costs on the wane, we saw our operating expenses as a percentage of sales come down to 19.5 percent. In fact, in the five years we discontinued advertising, we had the highest gains in same-store sales in our segment of retailing, and maybe in all retailing. The truth was we had better sales when we stopped advertising! They were better than the sales of our competitors who continued to advertise. We understood our customer, who bought when she needed something, at the best price she could find. If she didn't need it, a lower price wasn't going to entice her to buy it.

Lower everyday prices increased sales. It was a gutsy—and scary—move to undertake, and it proved to be very profitable. In January 1998, total sales were up by 27.6 percent, and same-store sales by 19.98 percent.

There was a lot more going on. We added a whole new department, nonperishable food, to our stores, resulting in the reconfiguration of every store in the company—2,700 stores in the first six months alone. We installed scanners at the checkouts, which helped with checkout speed and accuracy. They helped with one aspect of shrinkage—you couldn't ring up an item at a lower price, for instance—although it was still possible to bypass the register altogether.

The scanners were part of a move to position new technology throughout the company to prepare for more growth, which was well under way—we opened a record number of new stores and a new distribution center that year. It was a performance I didn't think anybody else in the business could have pulled off, and I said so in our annual report.

If eliminating advertising was counterintuitive, perhaps a merchandising strategy we inaugurated at the time was too. We decided to reduce the number of items with high profit margins, mainly clothing. In their place came lower-margin but faster-selling general merchandise such as paper towels and detergents. We also added hundreds of so-called consumable items, mainly snack foods, to increase customer traffic. We more than doubled the number of items we carried in each store and narrowed our profit margins, but the increased sales more than compensated. At first, we couldn't stock the shelves fast enough, but once we got that part of the equation down, we enjoyed yet another boost in profits.

In March 1998, we reported that same-store sales for February were up 22 percent and Dollar General stock jumped 6½ percent on the news. The next morning we made the *The Wall Street Journal.* I called my dad and I could hear the tears of joy in his voice as I told him. The company was doing better than he could ever have imagined. We carried $1.5 billion in inventory and had spent $75 million just on capital improvements that year. They were unbelievable numbers given where he'd come from. My dad still looked at sales figures, and he was as proud of Dollar General as he had ever been. He was eighty-two and frailer than I liked, but he was full of enthusiasm for the company. Thanks to the great run we were on, I was just as enthusiastic.

16

❧

Selective Unscrewing

We hadn't mentioned vendors in our company mission statement, but we knew they were critically important to our success. My dad always considered them to be partners in delivering greater value to our struggling customers. He wanted the relationship to be cooperative—we should not engage in the typical retailer's gamesmanship when it came to negotiating with vendors.

Our number one vendor at the time was Procter & Gamble, one of the world's largest and best-known corporations, and one day P&G's chairman, John Pepper, came to our Nashville office to meet with our executives and thank us for our business. John wanted to explore opportunities for an even better relationship. He asked for some one-on-one time with me, and I thought about how far Dollar General had come and how pleased Luther Turner would have been that a Turner's opinions would be of interest to that kind of corporate leader! The meeting signaled that we had grown enough for them to want a real partnership.

John looked as if he had come out of Central Casting. He was impeccably dressed, polished, and dignified, with gray hair and glasses. He was buttoned down and a bit formal; something made me want to tweak that, to bring a little of the Turner earthiness to bear on our conversation.

I was in the habit of giving my executives study Bibles. I chose the unusual gesture of giving one to him, and then said, "John, would you like to know the real strategic genius of Dollar General?"

"Yes," he said, looking very interested. "What is it, Cal?"

"Well," I told him, "our past has always been screwed up, and every year, we just selectively unscrew a bit."

That certainly put a different expression on his face. I could almost see him thinking, *How on earth do I react to that?*

Behind the "irreverence" of my statement, there was a point I wanted to make: The strategic secret of Dollar General lies in its past. We freely admit we have never operated our company to its full potential, and management is genuinely interested in learning the truth from frontline employees who experience and analyze company problems firsthand. One of the finest examples of that came when we decided to tinker with one of our best-sellers—a three-pack of microwave popcorn that sold for $1. "Let's give them an eight-pack for two dollars," we said, and that's what we did. We figured customers couldn't resist the added value, and we'd be generating a $2 sale instead of a $1 sale. The problem was that popcorn sales fell. Nobody could figure out why it wasn't a big success. We finally went into the stores and asked, and our people there told us our customers could only afford to spend $1 at a time for something like popcorn. We had lost some of our essential understanding of our customers, an understanding our store employees still had.

All companies have problems. The progressive ones develop the management and culture to solve problems holistically. Every year, we improve a little bit, and a little bit of improvement at a company like Dollar General is powerful.

In order to understand Dollar General and the Turner family's way of thinking about life and business, John was going to have to see the common sense and ego management that grounded us. He was proffering all of Procter & Gamble's finely honed logistical prowess to a company whose cofounder used to say, "Shucks! The only inventory control I have is the four walls of my warehouse!" because he couldn't buy any more than he could fit inside. I knew that behind all the expertise and the closer ties they were offering, the bottom line was that this was a way for P&G to get more business from Dollar General—a potential win for both companies. In the brief time we had together, I wanted to cut through the formality and yet emphasize that our bottom line was doing more for our customers. I wanted every vendor, big or small, to know it had to support the relationship we had with our customers, which involved using low prices on consumable basics to help give them a better life.

P&G was looking to help us move merchandise through our stores faster, and they were promising to help with the supply side of that equation. They said we could get our inventory turn—the rate at which merchandise flows through the company—to six times a year. That meant with ninety-day terms—our vendors expected payment ninety days after we received the merchandise—we'd be selling merchandise before we paid for it! We'd never be out of stock, and we could sell more with less shelf space. Of course, we could fill that leftover shelf space with more P&G products.

The meeting and follow-up were helpful, and I do believe my Kentucky bluntness helped set the tone.

The concept of "unscrewing" has to do with change, and change is something most of us resist. It may be simple fear of the unknown, for we cling to the security of a predictable structure or pattern, although it's worth remembering that people also get bored with the predictable.

One of DG's consulting psychologists, Dr. Mortimer Feinberg, was interviewing the company's key leaders to learn what motivated them and help me figure out how to improve the company. At one point he said, "Cal, you've got a problem. Everybody loves you because you've made them rich. You're never going to get change in a company with everybody so rich, happy, and satisfied."

I said, "Mort, what you're missing is that if they love me, they want to please me, and they know that what excites and pleases me is change. How do we change the business in the right kind of way? What can we do next for our customer? What are the steps we can take together, working in sync?"

That's the unscrewing process, taking the next step in bettering your approach, and the key is teamwork. Done well, it's satisfying and fulfilling and everybody wants to be a part of it. That was how we had undertaken strategic planning. I had told our executives how much we needed them as we took Dollar General to the next level, and I told them the success we earned would be shared. Part of my personal mission at Dollar General was to give them the opportunity to get rich, which in my view involves both having financial resources and becoming a good steward of them. I'm interested in wealth that is empowered and committed to serving others.

Many people have trouble with the disparity between the paychecks of entry-level employees and those in leadership positions in big companies like Dollar General, and I'd be remiss if I didn't address it. A straight-up comparison gives everyone, me included, heartburn, and yet it doesn't address the realities of the marketplace, where business success or failure occurs. Most new businesses fail, and not even longevity is a guarantor of continued success. Twentieth-century retail giants with long track records of success, such as A&P, G. C. Murphy, and F. W. Woolworth, went under.

Our aim as a company was to provide our often-struggling customers with the lowest-cost merchandise possible. That meant keeping our costs down, and salaries were our single largest expense. When Dollar General had 6,000 stores and 60,000 employees, at least a third of those were entry level. Giving each of them a $1-per-hour raise would have cost $40 million per year. While his or her compensation is much higher, there is only one CEO, and that person is tasked with and judged by total company performance.

We wanted to increase the salaries of entry-level employees by helping them move up the ladder, from stock person to assistant store manager, from store manager to district manager, and so on. Good leadership develops programs to help people advance within the company, which involves assuming responsibility for the performance of more employees, and it's motivating for employees to see others rise through the ranks. It's worth noting that once someone rose to assistant store manager, the pay increased and he or she had access to our bonus and stock option plan.

Finally, the free market determines pay levels. There is much greater competition for those who can fill upper-level management positions and take on higher levels of responsibility, and in the marketplace, such competition is demonstrated with higher salaries and bonus plans. The success of the company is what leadership is all about, and rewarding those who enhance the company's success means the company will grow and serve more people—customers and employees alike.

As a corporation, Dollar General touched the lives of every element of society. Here we were talking about executives who made a lot of money and store employees we hoped would share in the challenges and rewards of running the company. On the other end of the economic scale, we had customers who were often struggling. That's why our business model offered quality basic merchandise at low prices. We knew something else we could offer was our continued support of literacy programs, and one outgrowth of that effort is something I'm still proud of. We met with some volunteers who ran a day care program in the neighborhood of Nashville's Sam Levy housing project. They said they would love to give out gift certificates redeemable in Dollar General stores to people enrolled in their adult literacy programs. As we talked about the challenges they faced, we realized that for all of our thousands of stores, there wasn't one close enough for them to shop. Conventional wisdom said we'd be crazy to put a store in a depressed, high-crime neighborhood. We'd lose our shirt. Yet few residents of the project had transportation to our stores. They were basically trapped. We recognized that for the shame it was and started talking about what a store like ours might contribute to the neighborhood. Primarily, it could provide real value. People there couldn't buy anything like the merchandise Dollar General carried at the prices we offered. Second, our desire to draw our employees from our customer base meant we'd be bringing one of the things this neighborhood most desperately needed—jobs. Since this literacy program was really about work literacy, a working store was the best thing we could offer the program. Students could learn on the job, and the neighborhood residents could be taking ownership of the store. This was a chance to offer real help in the form of paychecks. They had day care, and transportation wasn't an issue, since we'd bring the jobs and training to where they lived. This had the potential to be a real success story, and we began to get excited about it.

We wanted to start out quietly. No press. No publicity. We knew this was a store with big failure prospects, and as a public company, we wanted the option to close it if it didn't work. Making a lot of noise about the opening would make it very difficult to do that. As excited as we were, we were also nervous.

We opened in 1993, and it wasn't long before the YWCA expressed interest in working with us. We teamed up with them— they even invested in the store—and the program grew under them. In fact, things went well for nearly four years. Then, in the midst of unrest that followed the fatal shooting of a resident by a police officer, the store was looted and burned. It was a huge disappointment to lose this symbol of private-public partnership in a neighborhood that sorely needed this kind of business presence.

After some deliberation, I am happy to say that we rolled up our sleeves and rebuilt the store. During the years it was open, more

17

My Dad's Final Years: Still Thinking About the Customer

Though I was no longer working with my dad, he remained proud of the company and of my role in it. He had a regular breakfast meeting with old friends at a local diner, and now and then he would arrive in a coat and tie rather than his normal casual clothes. That meant I was going to be in Scottsville and we'd be getting together. "The boss is coming to town," he would proudly tell his friends. He was living out his longtime contention that your dress reflects the respect you are showing the other person.

I treasured my time with him more than ever. Our relationship had changed, yet we both wanted the deep connection we'd always had. He had lost a great deal. His grief over the loss of his lifetime sweetheart had an effect on everything he did. I believe if Mama had lived longer, he would have been better able to accept the changes that had to happen with the transformation of the company from family business to professionally run organization. As it was, his removal from the company and the loss of Steve from its management continued to affect him. Business was synonymous with family, and these were tough blows.

He was more emotional in those years. He had always been quick to express emotion, with his anger rising and expressing itself suddenly, then dissipating just as quickly, but good and bad were both closer to the surface as he got older. Our disagreements had always tapped into those emotions, and one of the biggest changes he faced was that he was no longer the boss. His position on any issue was not necessarily the company's position. He had to adapt to that change and to the fact that his take on an issue or a decision, no matter how emotionally charged, had less effect than it once did.

Yet it was touching to watch him deal with his displacement and the way he reached out for family contact and reassurance. He was lonesome and wanted companionship and so at one point he surveyed all four kids, looking for permission to ask a family friend for a dinner date. Faye York and her late husband, Ira, had been good friends to both our parents. My dad wanted us to know that his lifetime sweetheart would always be Laura Katherine, but he wanted to feel comfortable spending time with Faye. The friendship of the four of them made him feel as if he had Laura Katherine's approval, and now he wanted ours. Of course, we gave it to him.

Without the pressures of work, my dad came around on the subject of philanthropy. He'd always considered work far more important than civic or charitable endeavors. "You have to work the store," he had said. "You don't have time for the Rotary Club." Toward the end, that changed to the extent that at one point he said, "Son, isn't it fun to give it away?"

In 1998, he asked the local ministerial association for a list of every church in Allen County. They couldn't come up with one, so he asked around, finally getting one from the rural electric co-op. Once he had it, he gave each of those churches $1,000. There were ninety-one of them, and for about half of them, his gift represented the single largest contribution they'd ever had. Heartfelt thank-yous poured in, and my dad, in a statement that displayed both his appreciation for small towns and his love of a good deal, said, "Son, look at what a bargain I got. You can't get this kind of gratitude in Nashville for ninety-one thousand dollars." In fact, he liked it so much that in early 2000 he did it again.

The 1990s came to a close with the company doing spectacularly well. Strategic planning and the board and management team we had in place positioned us to take full advantage of the decade's boom. By 2000, Dollar General was one of the best-performing public retailers, and the dollar store sector was the one strong growth venue of retailing, primarily because of what Dollar General was doing. Many other companies had tried to copy us, but we were still outpacing them. We had earnings increases of more than 15 percent for thirty-seven consecutive quarters. Only one other company, Cisco Systems, could equal that performance.

By this time, looking forward meant giving thought to a succession plan. I had been president of the company for twenty-three years, and had been chairman, CEO, and COO for much of that time. Those four posts would have been held by at least three people almost anywhere else. I was in no hurry to step aside, and I was reluctant to fill the post of COO, which was Steve's last company role, but I knew it was time to begin the process of greater succession planning. In March 2000, we named Bob Carpenter, someone I knew well and trusted, president and COO. I was also hopeful about our CFO, someone we wanted to groom for senior management. While he wasn't a financial person as such, we felt he had the leadership skills the company needed. Besides, we had a vice president/controller with a solid retail accounting background reporting to him. With those executives in place, we looked at a number of ways of improving our operations. We jump-started distribution, expanding our warehouse capacity to support growth in existing territories. Our distribution centers could handle about 700 stores each, and we wanted to get that number to 1,000. Inside those centers, our technology was state-of-the-art, but we wanted to stretch it further. We needed to be able to coordinate customer checkout, store ordering, and perpetual stock inventory as we sought to move goods through the stores ever more efficiently.

We were resetting every store, widening and rearranging aisles and wall displays in an effort to improve merchandise presentation, and we were rethinking what we carried, tweaking merchandise assortments as different items did well or poorly. Thanks to the new scanners we installed in every store in just six weeks, we were speeding up checkout as well. Meanwhile, we opened 239 stores in the first quarter of 2000.

That year, Dad developed jaundice and the doctors discovered that his bile duct was blocked. He underwent the first surgery of his eighty-four years as they went in and did a diversion. We were worried about the kind of patient he would be, since Turners aren't great patients anyway, but he surprised us all. His attitude was remarkably upbeat.

About two months later, the jaundice returned and we made arrangements for more tests in Nashville. The morning we were to drive down, he was ready to go into the office for a couple of hours of work beforehand.

"Son," he said when he saw the concern on my face, "you ought to jump into some work. It will take your mind off your troubles."

For so many years, people had worried about the negative effect work might be having on him, and here he was making it clear that it had been a great help to his mental and, no doubt, physical well-being.

The doctor called soon afterward and said Dad had cancer of the bile duct and probably had about a year to live. I was devastated. He got to his office, and Earline Frost, who had been my secretary but had become his when the rest of us moved to Nashville, said, "Mr. Turner, I am praying for a miracle."

"Earline," he said, "my life has already been a miracle. God does not owe me anything."

I had to face the fact that we were going to lose him. He, on the other hand, told me that he was worried about how hard I was working. Talk about a reversal! He knew the pressures that went with running the company, and he worried about the load I carried. It was time for me to channel him. "Daddy," I said, echoing what he'd said over and over through the years, "hard work won't kill you. It's actually good for you!"

He had long since been gone from active decision making, but I made sure he was able to keep his office so he could still feel involved to some degree, and he went there every day. He always related in a very personal way to everything going on in every one of our stores, and that was a big part of what kept him going after Mama died.

At the end of one of our meetings in Scottsville, as I was about to drive back to Nashville, he stood almost deferentially to say goodbye to me. He put his hand on the tall desk chair, cleared his throat, and with tears streaming down his face, said, "Son, thank you for prolonging my life."

I could tell how grateful he was for our support of him and the recognition of the importance of his contributions to the company. People esteemed what he said in board meetings because of that support and recognition, and while I had never thought about that as prolonging his life, it was a very sweet thing for a father to say to his son.

We'd had our troubles through the years, but as the end drew near, his words to me didn't come in the form of "ought" or "should," but in terms of love and hope.

"Cal Jr.," he said, "I hope you will be as good a father and grandfather as you have been a son."

He saw my tears. He understood the emotion behind them, a soul-wrenching sadness at losing my mentor in life and business, my dear and longest friend. Still, the hope that infused our conversations was more powerful than the sorrow. I would carry something wonderful forward.

My siblings and I prepared for the inevitable. Steve and I had come a long way in repairing our relationship, and we and our two sisters took a great deal of solace in one another. We gathered at the family home in Kentucky and had wonderful discussions with Daddy, who expressed his utter joy with the life he'd lived and thanked each of us for our part in it. At one point, he regarded us for a long moment and said softly, "Thank you for making my life a heaven on earth." He was just as grateful for the community that had nurtured him, and for the business to which he'd given his life. Still, he was very ready for the end to come.

We were talking about his funeral one day. We agreed the high school was the only building in town that could accommodate the crowds we expected. The gym seemed the logical place, with any overflow going to the auditorium.

"Wait a minute," said Dad. "There may not be enough people to fill it, and you may be embarrassed. Why don't we have it in the auditorium? It's smaller and you're more guaranteed of overflow!"

Another time, we were discussing whether to have an open or a closed casket at the funeral.

"There'll be a lot of people coming from out of town," he said. "For some, it will be a long drive, and they may not be able to come for the visitation. If you don't open the casket at the funeral, they won't get their money's worth."

He was still thinking about the customer.

One day a florist came to the house with ninety-one red roses addressed to him. It was as heartwarming a thing as I'd ever seen. We had roses everywhere. They had obviously been sent by someone touched by his $1,000 contributions to each of the ninety-one churches in Allen County.

My dad looked at them and said, "We need to send some of these to our church, and some to the Baptist church," and he named several other people and churches. Of course, by "we," he meant his kids, and we went all over town delivering flowers.

A week later, less than a week before he died, I talked him into one last ride in the car. He fell asleep in the passenger seat beside me now and then, but at one point he suddenly roused and said, "Turn here." It was a country road I had never even noticed before. We wound around two or three curves and he said, "There's a church over there." It was one of the ninety-one, and it sat in the autumn sun, as still and peaceful a picture as I had ever seen.

He said, "Son, I never knew this church was here until we did our research. I have lived in Allen County for more than seventy-five years. That church was here before I came and it will be here long after I'm gone. But while I was here, I had the joy of being part of its ministry."

That was what philanthropy meant at the end to a man who once said, "You can't afford to do that. If there's any philanthropy in you, it's in your work and in your business, because that's how you're going to provide for your family. You have to do that first." Now he wanted the money he'd made to be useful to people in the place where their deepest needs met their dearest hopes.

I remember sitting in his bedroom with Margaret and my dad's nurse. He was unconscious and struggling for breath. He wished for an immediate death, but his body, so used to working, so driven to move forward, was set on living. It was laboring, taking breath after breath despite the awful pneumonia he'd developed.

The end came on November 14, 2000. The esteem in which he was held by everyday people and by the nation's business leaders was evident. Mourners from both worlds packed the high school auditorium for the funeral, and the overflow filled half the gym. His passing was noted in publications ranging from the local paper to *The New York Times*.

"Cal Turner, Sr., was one of the giants of retailing, one of the original founders of mass retailing, a true leader, a visionary," said Robert Verdisco, president of the International Mass Retail Association. "Someone like him doesn't come around very often. The loss to our industry cannot be measured, and there are few who have done so much."

It was the month of Thanksgiving, and I was profoundly grateful for the life of this man who had done more for me than any other person alive. He was known by those who encountered him as a genuinely humble, self-effacing individual driven by the value of hard work. He often admitted that he didn't really feel he had ever had any truly original ideas. Rather, he confessed that his success could be attributed to learning from others and implementing their successful ideas.

It had worked. As the founder of a family business that launched the dollar store segment of retailing, he left an incredible personal and business legacy.

18

⋙⋘

Exiting the Company: That Lonesome Valley

I didn't get the time I needed to deal with my father's death. About a month before he died, I received a memo stating that there were problems in our accounting department. It's the kind of thing you never want to hear, but at first I wasn't unduly alarmed. It had come from a few rungs down the executive ladder, so I asked the company's president and its CFO to look into the matter. I was dealing with my father's illness and death. In fact, much of that year end was a blur for me.

Someone under our controller was alleging accounting irregularities. I believed in the controller's integrity and the charges didn't make sense to me, but the memo had torn a little hole in the fabric of the company that was getting larger every day.

We issued a press release and held a conference call with analysts on January 22, 2001, announcing that earnings for 2000 were lower than expected. Meanwhile, I asked the CFO of a Nashville-based company with a nationwide presence, someone with retailing experience, to join us as CFO and help us get straightened out. Once he agreed, we installed him and let our then-CFO go. It was the appropriate move, but it also took the situation to another level. Our fired CFO made allegations of improper practices within the company and asked for a hearing before the board's audit committee. Instead, on April 12, we brought together senior management and our SEC counsel, and the fired CFO and his attorney presented a laundry list of complicated charges that involved the misreporting of inventory values, the mislabeling of leases in financing new stores, unreconciled bank statements, and more. The incredible thing was that we all were listening to the former CFO of the company, the man ultimately responsible for our financial integrity and compliance, suggesting things were terribly wrong in his own accounting department!

These were serious and complicated charges that needed to be turned over to the lawyers and forensic accountants, and I knew once that happened, management would be emasculated in terms of dealing with them. I talked to our SEC counsel, who said, "Cal, you stay out of this. Let me handle it. My firm will come in and investigate."

They did, and with a vengeance. My first stark discovery of the fact that this problem was going to be about me as well as the company came when our counsel told me I needed my own personal attorney.

"But my interest isn't different from the company's," I said.

"Yes it is," he said. "Where this is going, you're going to need your own lawyer." He gave me the name of an attorney and told me to call him. I did, retaining him before we met and before we had even discussed what was going on.

We had a board meeting coming up a few days later. The company counsel was going before the board to give a report damaging to me and other senior management, which technically put him in a conflict of interest. That's why he wanted me represented separately. He was representing the company, but he was going to be casting me, as CEO, in a bad light. I wasn't present at the meeting, but as I expected, the report found fault with senior management and with me. After receiving it, the board decided to retain new counsel, hiring Ralph Ferrara of Debevoise & Plimpton in Washington, D.C.

We hired an army of lawyers and accountants from several top firms to come in and start going over the books. As often happens, they were all eager to outdo one another and earn their keep by finding things that were wrong or out of place. Everybody seemed to have a stake in making us look bad. The process was terribly injurious and punitive, and a lot of people were getting hurt.

Two hours before the next board meeting, Ralph and our top company counsel came into my office and suggested that I resign at the meeting. They said that my doing so would make it easier to deal with the SEC, would show that I and the company were taking the matter seriously, and would make it easier for the company to make other tough management decisions. I was stunned. I had been CEO for thirty-five years, and now they were saying I had two hours to make a decision about whether or not to step down. I didn't say no. I simply told them that two hours was not enough time to process and make a decision like that.

It did give me plenty to think about. I worked under the long-standing assumption that my job was to fix whatever was wrong with the company. It was what my father had wanted when I signed on. It gave him breathing room, and it was what I planned to do here.

I saw great irony in the fact that my dad had once told me, "Son, you're always going to have a surprise at year's end." His bookkeeping system was an attempt to make it a positive surprise, offsetting shrinkage. Now, here we were with a huge fulfillment of his prediction—an accounting shock yet to play out fully. He was right. It burst one bubble I'd had—the thought that we had managed the company beyond such surprises. Maybe it was an endemic flaw in my father's business that as CEO I had to admit I had failed in achieving thorough, professional management that wouldn't fall prey to such surprises.

On April 30, we issued a press release announcing the discovery of accounting irregularities. We said we would be restating our audited financial statements for the years 1998, 1999, and 2000, and those statements would reflect lower earnings.

The SEC's entry into the matter had taken it to yet another level. Their responsibility is to protect shareholders, and they are charged with uncovering wrongdoing, so their reports invariably emphasize the negative. The SEC's involvement sets in motion a very dramatic and very public chain of events. In fact, the way the system works, the cure can often be worse than the disease; doctoring the patient can sometimes kill it. The process of forensic accounting and legal investigation adds a major financial cost and can just take the heart out of a company, especially one so dedicated to its customers, its employees, and its values. A company with a harsh management style experiencing a financial restatement would probably not face the same threat to its existence as a company with the soft, people-centered approach that made Dollar General successful.

The SEC complaint charged that the company had underreported $10 million in freight expense, overstated cash accounts, and manipulated earnings through a rainy-day account. It alleged that I personally "knew of serious allegations concerning [our controller] and was reckless in not knowing that these issues were likely to impact the integrity and accuracy of Dollar General's financial statements." It said our actions were "motivated in part by a desire to report earnings that met or exceeded analysts' expectations and to maintain employee bonuses."

Investigators went over our books and memos and took depositions all through the year, and on January 14, 2002, we released our audited restated financial statements for 1998 to 2000, reflecting dramatic reductions in income. The restated figures for 2000 showed $70.6 million in net income and $0.21 in diluted earnings per share versus $206 million and $0.62, respectively. We recognized a pretax expense of $162 million in the second quarter of 2000, reflecting the settlement we reached in class action and derivative lawsuits arising from the restatements.

I was able to say in the annual report announcing all this, "We have never had an unprofitable year in our company's history, and this was only the fifth year-over-year earnings decline," but that was of little comfort to stockholders. Our stock had dropped from $23 to less than $16 and it would continue to decline, sliding before long into single digits. Tens of billions of dollars of wealth disappeared, and the fortunes of literally thousands of Dollar General families were cut by nearly two-thirds.

We announced that the large-scale changes we were undertaking in 2000, from resetting every store to adding 239 new ones, had been "overwhelming" to us as a company, but it was the restatement that overshadowed everything. There is no way to overstate the importance of that event. The credibility of a public company lies in the financial reports it gives to shareholders, and ours was on the line. When it was first announced, some people said, "Well, it's obvious they were cooking the books." It was a statement that hit way below the belt for someone who had been a values-based leader. One long-standing shareholder was quoted as saying, "It feels like my beloved dog has died." He felt Dollar General was that wonderful, and when you're deemed wonderful and you foul up, suddenly you become worse than bad.

This was a company that had come through a dozen years of incredible growth and success. In just the five-year period beginning in 1997, we had opened 3,025 stores, more than half of the 5,540 stores in the chain, seen sales double from $2.7 billion to $5.3 billion, and added five million square feet of distribution center space to the two million we had. For a company with that kind of track record and that kind of continued success, having to air such terribly dirty linen in public just after my dad's death was an incredibly tough event to witness. I was so glad it had not occurred while my father was there to see it. The son he viewed as his shining star was presiding over events that reflected very badly on the integrity that had been such a part of building the company.

I missed him terribly. I had often joked when I excused myself from some meeting or function that "I must leave to be about my father's business." I was playing both with the scriptural reference (Luke 2:49) and the fact that it was in a very real sense my dad's company. He was Cal Sr., "the real Cal Turner," as I sometimes said. I was Cal Jr. I had always drawn on him as a resource, and now I couldn't.

I recalled the differences in our management styles as reflected in some of our conversations. When something went wrong, he used to ask, "Who did that?" My approach was different: "Daddy, I'm not going to tell you who did it. The important response is, 'What happened and who needs help to fix it?'"

It became part of who we were as a company. In one of the intense self-evaluations we did during the days when we were first implementing strategic planning, our statement of values became, "We believe in building our company with persons who have a living commitment to moral integrity, who have a sense of personal mission, who value work and other people, who believe in developing human potential by emphasizing strengths in a blame-free environment where performance gaps are processed in a way that develops the team and the person."

It was a statement that was all-encompassing as to principle and purpose. Now, though, with Cal Sr. dead, I was tempted to ask his question: "Who did this dastardly thing?"

Where I could act, though, I had to see if I had what it took to get past blame to constructive action. I had to own the failure, especially the incentive and bonus compensation structure. That had put excessive pressure on everyone throughout the company to attain profit objectives. Earnings per share triggered the bonuses and stock options of everyone from assistant store managers to the CEO. In a 6,000-store chain, that is a lot of people. In my mind, it was a noble thing to do. It was the ultimate statement of our being in this as a team. And yet, it put such emotion-laden, gut-churning emphasis on achieving that number that some good people did things that were wrong.

I had some real processing to do. I was going to have to dig deeply into myself. The issue was how to handle myself in the way that would produce the best outcome for everybody. There were a lot of people hurt, and that was especially painful to me because I was still hurting from the loss of my dad. I had also lost power in the company. I felt as though I'd lost credibility. Everybody was looking at me differently. People within the company weren't sure how to relate to me. I was relating to myself differently, for that matter.

I had lost much of my company identity, and yet I was still dealing with the SEC. The investigations and public announcements, the depositions, findings, and settlements continued. I had to go through hours and hours of grilling by lawyers and prepare myself for my time in the barrel at the SEC.

It's one thing to have a tough situation and know what you have to do. I had already faced the toughest imaginable situations and walked through them once I had determined the right course of action. This was different. I didn't have any idea how to handle it. I would need someone to talk to besides the company lawyers.

I especially valued the opinions of two directors, David Wilds and John Holland, so I consulted both of them. In-house, I talked to Bob Carpenter and Stonie O'Briant, one of our executive vice presidents. I would go to one who would emphatically recommend one course of action, and another who would recommend something else.

I got great support from Margaret. It was wonderful having a loving partner at a time like that. Still, as she had never been involved in the business, it was not easy for her to understand all the intricacies of the company, of the SEC, of all the legal and financial things going on. The conversations I had with her and with my fellow executives brought some benefit, but all were incomplete. No one had the big picture, the complete overview of Dollar General as a family-business-turned-public company, the kind of perspective that went with longevity and deep insight.

No one, that is, except my brother, Steve. In the absence of my dad, he had more knowledge and insight than anybody. It had been a dozen years since I'd fired him. We had dealt with each other on better terms, especially in the days before and after Daddy's death, although there was still a great deal of space between us. Maybe honest and open conversation with him would re-cement more of the bonds we'd had as brothers. I decided to talk with him.

I didn't go in expecting much help, but I was trying to achieve some additional bonding. I had lost my brother and my dad, and I was in the process of losing the company. I wanted to regain my brother as much as possible. We sat down a couple of times and he was sympathetic to my need to process all that had gone on. He didn't know the ins and outs, but he understood that in the absence of our father, his older brother needed love and support from him, the younger. I could sense that he was trying to do just that, and yet I knew that his feelings about our differences still had to be in the background.

The meeting was congenial and Steve was sympathetic, but there had been an ironic switching of roles. Steve had always been the one to debate and I had been the one to counsel and console. Now I needed his counsel and consolation. I have to give him high marks for his valiant effort to offer both, but neither of us was quite right for the roles we were trying to fill here. Temperamentally, I was a Turner. He was a Goad. We both missed the real Cal Turner. It would have been natural for our father to act as the catalyst for the healing that needed to happen. To some degree he could have helped Steve and me relate better to each other. I was glad he had been spared all this, but his absence made for a great deal of pathos in that meeting.

I went in to testify before the SEC, and as they fired questions at me, I was able to find an emotional anchor in a memory of Mr. Jimmy's Sunday vespers at Camp Dunroamin. I thought about lighting my candle, saying, "The Lord is my light and my salvation. Whom shall I fear?" I could see Mr. Jimmy on the other side of the candle, and the thought brought me real peace in the midst of a truly terrible session.

Sometimes you have to walk that lonesome valley by yourself, and this would be one of those times. I knew nothing was going to be the same from here on out. It was time to find out how the best future for Dollar General could be crafted out of all the pain and carnage—and what my role in that future was to be. There was a new ingredient in my thinking, one that had come by way of the lawyers. It was a startling revelation—that at this point, the best way to fix the company was to realize that perhaps I wasn't the one to fix it. For the first time in thirty-seven years, the solution might not involve me.

Once I got past the shock, the newness of it, I came to believe that the right course of action would be extricating myself from Dollar General management. That would enable the company to reconstruct its future without me. It would be best for everybody.

During the years I led Dollar General, the thing I always hated most was firing people. I never got comfortable with it, and I often thought it would be poetic justice if someday I had to fire myself. That's just how I look now at what happened. I had begun to feel pressure from the SEC attorneys we hired to prepare me for the hearings. I had said no to their request, just before that board meeting, that I submit my resignation, but now I could see the value in that option. The board committee dealing with SEC matters was still exerting pressure, but ultimately, the decision was mine. As painful as it was, in September 2002, I stepped down as CEO. Donald Shaffer served as interim CEO until April 2003, when former Reebok president David Perdue became CEO, with Shaffer continuing as COO. I remained board chairman until June. That month, we instituted the last major change under my watch, opening the first Dollar General

19

⋙⋘

Retirement: Redefining
Who I Am

In August 2011, I attended the funeral of Walter Gupton, Dollar General's longtime number one operations person and the man who had sent me to open my second store, in Anniston, Alabama, with someone even greener at opening stores than I was. The funeral was held at a little country church, and as I stood outside with two former district managers, I told the story of that Anniston opening.

"Well," said one of the managers, "that's not the way it was. Here's what really happened." And he proceeded to tell the story with a decidedly different mix of facts and quotations.

I had ridden to the church with the other manager, and as he and I headed back to town, he said, "Well, that lying SOB. That's not the way it happened at all!" And he went through *his* recollection.

I had always thought my version was the sacred history of what had happened, and I had told it from time to time with the authority of a CEO. Now, I realized that mine was just one of at least three equally "authoritative" versions.

Truth, it turns out, is a bit different for everybody. It's why most of us are notoriously unreliable witnesses. Our versions are shaded by the emotions of the time. There is no complete truth on earth—there is simply each person's version of that truth.

This book has looked through my eyes at the events that entwined

238 • MY FATHER'S BUSINESS

my life with the story of Dollar General. It is my story, my truth, written from the position of retirement, a time in life I've given great consideration. My greatest insight about retirement lies in the first few verses of my favorite chapter in the Bible, Romans 12. Retirement is our last opportunity to present our bodies as living sacrifices, as death is more imminent than ever. My thought is that God-centered processing of our lives and their meaning is the greatest of all opportunities in retirement, and Romans 12 tells us how: "Be not conformed to this world, but be transformed by the renewing of your mind that you may prove what the will of God is, that which is good and acceptable and perfect." Our greatest and last chance for creative partnership with God comes in retirement. It is also our best opportunity for serving others, who learn more from what we model than from what we message.

I see this as a time of reflection, a haven outside the events of a working life from which to look back with new perspective, as observer rather than participant. From this vantage, I see more of the hand of God in my life, guiding me through the good and the bad, especially when events forced me toward earnest prayer and deep reflection, as they did in that fateful season when the family and company were split in 1987 and 1988.

Retirement has given me the opportunity to review the lessons of a lifetime, and to reestablish my connection to the Cal Jr. who really began his spiritual journey, which happened to coincide by and large with his family's retail journey, at age eleven. My relationship with Jesus Christ remains an integral part of who I am—"a practicing, backsliding Methodist." For Jesus Christ himself is the ultimate standard and that is the point of reference from which we are backsliding! Backsliding in that sense has become a virtue to me, for its standard of measurement is God himself. It is also a great way to practice ego management, because when you think of yourself as a practicing backslider, you're willing to reach out for help and support from others, and that brings people together.

It is my hope in writing this book that you can be inspired to pursue your mission. I hope you will find ways to use your gifts for the betterment of those around you, always striving to close that gap between aim and achievement, but accepting that as humans we will never do so perfectly.

We are all works in progress. In retirement, we may have set aside day-to-day career pursuits. We may have tied our working lives up with a bow. Still, God is not through with us until we walk through that final portal. We can retire from meetings, from work e-mails, from the stresses of new products and bottom lines, but we can't retire from the much more important tasks of living—spiritual growth and serving others.

My mission statement remains "God-honoring change," and I believe there is continuity between the way I tried to carry it out as an executive and the way I do so now as a retired person. A mission statement should open us to greater possibilities, and there are as many of those now as there ever have been.

Several things have given me meaning in retirement. For starters, there is philanthropy, something I view in its broadest sense. It is poor philanthropy indeed that is measured only in dollars and cents. Each of us has time, energy, talent, and experience, and I believe we are called to share all of those things for the betterment of others.

As CEO of Dollar General, I was especially drawn to the cause of literacy. It was one of the issues facing our struggling customers, and it was close to my heart because of my grandfather Luther Turner's third-grade education. I remain chairman of the board of the Dollar General Literacy Foundation, which since its inception in 1993 has awarded more than $125 million in grants to nonprofit organizations, including Dolly Parton's Imagination Library and the (Tennessee) Governor's Books from Birth Foundation, and has helped nearly eight million individuals take their first steps toward literacy or continued education.

The word *philanthropy* stems from the Greek words for "love of your fellow man." I believe God put philanthropic DNA in everyone, but it can take many different forms. At one end of the spectrum, there is elevator philanthropy, that quick affirming connection you can make with someone you'll see just once during a ten-second elevator ride. At the other is a lifetime of service to people and causes, bringing every part of your being into the process.

And this would be a good place to state that few people are more qualified to speak about philanthropy than my brother, Steve. Once he was independent of the company, he went on to major success in his own right. He was liberated to perform and succeed and got engaged in all kinds of charitable endeavors. He has been a major force in philanthropy in our community of Nashville, and I'm proud of him for that.

He and I joined forces in supporting the effort to build a symphony hall befitting our beloved second home, a city known for music that already had a great symphony orchestra. Our friend Martha Ingram took the lead, and we were happy to join her in supporting the arts in this way. We knew it would be a major asset to the community, and it had a wonderful resonance for me, given my lifelong love of music. I took great joy in the partnership I had with Steve on this project—it was brother bonding and community enhancing. The building was named the Schermerhorn Symphony Center, after longtime symphony conductor Kenneth Schermerhorn, and we took special pride in having named the Laura Turner Concert Hall in honor of our mother.

Then there is mentoring. Here, too, I think the term refers to far more than the narrow definition we often use. Mentoring is unique to every person and situation. It happens on a small scale every time one person models any positive behavior, from kindness to goal setting.

My appreciation for mentorship came from my being the beneficial recipient of it, as I saw my grandfather's eagerness to learn from everyone, my father's work ethic, my mother's emphasis on treating everyone with respect and her oh-so-healthy separation of the person from the problem. Throughout my years at Dollar General, I learned from my father, from Larry Appley, Wallace Rasmussen, John Holland, and others with great business and life lessons to share, and I learned from those on the front lines—the clerks and managers who made each store work. Throughout, my faith connected me with Christ, the ultimate role model and mentor.

What if, in taking responsibility and assessing our efforts to live up to that model, we come up short of the mark? I don't like the word *sin*, but I can embrace the word *failure*. Looked at correctly, failure is often a better mentor than success. I spoke a while back to seniors at Florida Southern College. They were nearing graduation, so I guessed they would all have their fears about the future. They may well have been expecting bromides, a "keep your chin up and it will all work out" sort of message. That's not what I gave them. I said, "What if you fail? Let's talk about that." I shared with them my experiences of failure and showed them how that was where I experienced the most growth.

The fear of failure is generally worse than the failure, and it teaches far fewer useful lessons, yet I don't think there's a mistake we can make that can't be useful to others. Many leaders in business, churches, and not-for-profits have some of the same tribulations to endure as mine. My aim is that my experience in retirement can help them while they're still mid-career. What I learned in times of joy and success was not nearly as helpful as what I learned in the bad times. Fortunately, both the good and the bad provide the opportunity to serve others.

One of the most crucial lessons I have learned about life and leadership is that the sense of purpose embodied in a mission statement is vital. Without a mission grounded in the perspective offered by a coherent worldview, we are simply corks floating in the sea of events around us. Until I fully know who I am and what my purpose is, my movement can be directionless.

It is never too late to reassess, to realign, to bring the focus of new perspective to bear on life. A great biblical example of a change of mission that worked wonders can be found in the thief on the cross. His life had clearly been a failure, and when we meet him, life is nearly over. But something in the eyes, words, and demeanor of Jesus convicted him. He was a changed man. He admonished the other thief, reminding him that Jesus was innocent, as they were not. Then he asked that Jesus remember him when he came into his kingdom.

"Truly, I say to you," Jesus said, "today you will be with me in Paradise."

Talk about being positioned for a great retirement! The thief wrapped his failure in a bow and embraced success. It shows that it's never too late to reevaluate and change direction, and that the rewards of doing so can be everlasting.

My look back can't be complete without my acknowledgment that Steve played his role in the company better than I would have. My dad played his role better than I would have as well. If I had more fully owned my ultimate impotence to fix the things that needed fixing in the company, I would perhaps have been positioned as a more graceful change agent. I had the "big brother" syndrome, and my determination to do the right thing as I saw it made me tough to live with for Steve.

My motive in this book has been to examine my father's business and make sense of it in a way that might invite you to do the same— so that you may help others to do the same in turn. It's part of loving others as ourselves.

Life is a stream. You come in with the contributions of everyone in the past behind you. You go into the stream and you accept their influence and add yours, alongside your contemporaries. When you die, you come out of the stream as yet others go in, with your influence going forward in those you have affected. Mission is taking seriously your opportunity to affect that stream while you're part of it, something we're all called to do.

You are one of a kind. That's why I've tried to share life lessons rather than offer advice. I can't offer better advice than you can glean for yourself, for only you know the life to which those lessons and advice can be applied. I or anyone sharing the lessons of experience can provide only a little sun, a little rain, a little fertilizer. Yours is the ground in which the seeds have been planted. I don't want to have gone through all of this without there being some benefit for others. That, too, is a Turner trait.

Each of us is best served by facing and learning—and relearning—the lessons of our lives and applying them anew each day. I acknowledge, by the way, that I'm the right person to talk about this process, because I'm still trying to figure it out myself.

God would have nothing to be wasted in any of our lives. I hope that sharing the good and the bad of my journey, the process of being about my father's business, can be helpful in your reflection on your journey, and in your continued progress toward more fulfillment as you seek to be about your Heavenly Father's business on earth.

INDEX

ABOUT THE AUTHORS

Cal Turner, Jr., grew up in a Scottsville, Kentucky, household where business and family were one. After graduating from Vanderbilt University, he served for three years as an officer in the United States Navy before beginning his career at Dollar General. He served as CEO for thirty-seven years, and during his tenure, the number of DG stores rose from 150, with sales of $40 million, to more than 6,000, with sales in excess of $6 billion. Turner has served on the boards of companies such as Shoney's and First American, and of educational, civic, and charitable organizations including Vanderbilt and Fisk Universities, and has been president of the board of governors of the Nashville Area Chamber of Commerce. His many awards include the Presidential Award for Private Sector Initiatives (presented by Ronald Reagan) and the Vanderbilt Distinguished Alumnus Award. A committed lifelong Methodist, Turner was inducted in 2001 into the Fellows of the Society of John Wesley by the Tennessee Conference of the UMC.

Rob Simbeck has written, edited, or contributed to more than twenty books. His work has appeared in dozens of publications, including *The Washington Post* and *Guideposts*. He lives and works in Nashville.